SERMONS FOR A HOT KITCHEN

FROM THE LESBIAN TENT REVIVAL

By Carolyn Gage

These sermons were originally given at the Michigan Womyn's Music Festival and the National Women's Music Festival between 2011 and 2015. The sermons on Holding Complexity and Confrontation were given in 2017 at the Michigan Framily Reunion. The sermons on stories, logotherapy and dying were podcast on the Internet.

Other collections by Sister Carolyn of the Sisterhood of the Sacred Synapse:

Sermons for a Lesbian Tent Revival

Supplemental Sermons for a Lesbian Tent Revival

Hotter Than Hell: More Sermons for a Lesbian Tent Revival

Testimonials from The Lesbian Tent Revival:

"The Lesbian Tent Revival—inspiring, encouraging, truth-telling, amazing, comedic, must-reading for all Radical Feminists. I never had so much fun as at the Tent Revivals at Michigan, being in a crowd of like-minded, laughing, singing, applauding and shouting-out with Sister Carolyn. She's pure genius. Buy This Book. You won't be sorry."—Susan Wiseheart

"... the absolute highlight! I had heard about it from a friend who attended last year, but still wasn't prepared for such a dazzling combination of clarity and humor. I can't think of a better way to get younger women thinking and reading and firing those synapses. Thanks so much for all you're doing to keep the dream alive-- it's truly an inspiration." -- April Applegate, Illinois.

"My sister sent me *Sermons for a Lesbian Tent Revival*. People often have a way with words, or a way with ideas, but seldom both. I read *Gynecology, Native Tongue, Cyborg Manifesto*, etc... but I can't say I was racked with laughter to balance the agony. I read your book in one sitting, like a glutton. It was the best read in years. You rock, Sister:)—Helena Saayaman, Pretoria, South Africa.

"The LTR rocked my world! In August at the MWMF my Aussie mates agreed that The LTR was our highlite and we left wanting more—much more. Clearly our weary les fem souls needed saving! Each morning Sister Carolyn delivered a riveting, inspiring and humourous sermon that made us sit up and think, laugh, cry."—Georgina Abrahams, Sydney, Australia

"I know that you brought back full circle what ... is in danger of being lost."—Maria Karpinski

Table of Contents

Preface

"If you can't take the heat, get out of the kitchen."

Well, that sounds like a good way to take care of yourself... until you realize that the kitchen is where it all happens. The kitchen is where the food is stored. The kitchen is where the appliances are for preparing it. The kitchen is where the magic happens. And, like as not, the kitchen is where the eating goes on.

And, of course, Sister Carolyn is not just talking about a literal kitchen... although that's a pretty important part of the house, and eating is a big piece of survival. But I am talking about your brain, your psyche, your thinking, your political and social and spiritual central command headquarters... the place up there between your ears. Sisters, what you got cookin'?

It just might be time to reconsider the price we pay for *not* taking the heat. Just how important is your comfort level when survival is on the line? And, sisters, if you are a lesbian, your survival is pretty much on the line every damn day. Because it's patriarchy out there. If you're doing it right, your kitchen is probably going to be hot.

Heat—thermal energy—happens when molecules and atoms bump up against each other, or else when vibrate back and forth. Are we bumping up against the world in ways that delight us, or that enrage us, or that terrify us? Are we positively vibrating with our own ideas, our own passion, our own creativity? Because we should be. It's called "being alive." And the more intensely we do that, the more heat we're going to generate.

With what's going on in the world today—and what's *not* going on in it—the kitchen between our ears should be *on fire* with energy. Sisters, there has never been so much opportunity—or so much atrocity. There has never been so much to be done. There has never been so much transformation so urgently needed. It's like we're all line cooks in the great restaurant of life, with those order tickets stacking up... only, instead of hearing, *"BLT!"* *"Blue plate special! Sunny side up!"* we're hearing, *"Climate change denial!"* *"Corruption in government!"* *"Polluted oceans!"*

Sisters, our mental kitchens should be hot—red hot! We all need to be cookin' up some kind of revolution... in ourselves, in the world.

And—yes—of course, there are times when we can't take the heat, when we just have to say, "That's enough for me. I'm out." But there's a lot to be said for increasing our tolerance for heat, for learning to focus on the job at hand, and for appreciating that the price of "getting it done" may be some personal discomfort. Maybe even a lot of personal discomfort.

So, sisters, let's take off our shirts and tie back our hair! Let's open all the damn windows and turn on the fans! Let's remind ourselves and others that this heat is what gets the job done.

Introduction

This is my fourth volume of Lesbian Tent Revival Sermons, and it contains sermons from 2012 through 2018. These have been seven interesting years in terms of the "Sisterhood of the Sacred Synapse," which is how "Sister Carolyn" refers to her beloved congregation at the Lesbian Tent Revival. (The Lesbian Tent Revival speaks to the ability of lesbians to think deeply and radically about our lives and how they have been affected by the patriarchy. At the Revival, this kind of synapsing is a sacrament.)

Anyway, these seven years that saw the end of the Michigan Womyn's Music Festival, which inspired the very first Revival in 2007, and which hosted nine years of Revivals up until 2015, when the Festival closed her gates for the last time. Every year, the Lesbian Tent Revival featured five days of different themes, with different sermons, for the week of the Festival. Five times nine is forty—forty Lesbian Tent Revivals on that blessed Land.

These last seven years also marked the final years of the Obama administration and the shocking election of Donald Trump. Perhaps not entirely unrelated, this last year has seen the rise of the #MeToo Movement, which appears to be one of the greatest watersheds in Western culture, heralding the end of women's tolerance for sexual harassment in the workplace—and especially within the privileged walls of the mainstream entertainment industry—that purveyor of dangerous and degrading stereotypes of women.

Some of these sermons came from those final years of the Festival, several are from a series of podcasts, and three were written after the Festival for other lesbian gatherings.

I begin this collection with the **Sermon on Prostitution**, which was inspired by Dr. Catharine MacKinnon, colleague of Andrea Dworkin, who is one of the "Saints" of the Lesbian Tent Revival, and who was one of my personal mentors. Dr. MacKinnon wrote an essay titled "Trafficking, Prostitution, and Inequality," which is so brilliant, I wanted to find a way to bring its substance to non-academic, but passionately feminist lesbians at the Festival.

I originally titled the sermon "How To Win Every Argument on Prostitution Every Time. Seriously." Because most of us have been frustrated when defenders of prostitution attempt to set the terms of the debate by framing prostitution abolitionists as oppressors of prostituted women, or else as "sex negative," self-appointed monitors of public morality.

Dr. MacKinnon systematically takes on every neoliberal construction of prostitution, destroying every argument— seriously—every time. I wrote the sermon to disseminate MacKinnon's brilliant approach, offering a powerful strategy for countering the widespread and intentional misinformation about prostitution.

I remember the day I gave this sermon. The heavens themselves opened up, pouring torrents of rain for nearly the entire hour. Few of us had brought raingear or tarps, and the water streamed down our faces, as the ground of the workshop turned into a field of mud. The pages of the sermon were so wet, they actually felted together, and it took the skill of a surgeon to separate them in such a way that they could still be read. I remember having to shout above the roar of the pounding rain. What I treasure about that Revival is this: The women stayed, because the issue was that important.

The next sermon in the collection is the **Sermon on Stories**, which spends a lot of time on the story of Sacagawea, the Native woman who enabled the Lewis and Clark Expedition to reach the Pacific Ocean. A wildly inaccurate account of her role has become enshrined in American frontier history as part of the heroic tale of the so-called "Opening the West." In fact, the true story is a testament to the horrors of racism and the genocide of indigenous peoples, the enslavement of abducted captives, the trafficking of native children, and the exploitation of women. There is, however, another story buried deep in Meriwether Lewis's famous journal. This is a radical and a feminist story, and it is why I wrote the sermon.

The **Sermon on Jealousy** is consistent with Sister Carolyn's commitment to the telling of family secrets, even when that family is our own lesbian-feminist one. Any longtime activist can testify to how divisive and potentially destructive jealousy can be in women's communities and organizations. In spite of that, there can be a powerful temptation to deny or refuse to confront this disruptive dynamic when it surfaces among our sisters. This sermon invites us to give our jealousies a hard and fair look.

The **Sermon on Mirrors and Firewalls** gives a name to two of the most potent invisible weapons that patriarchy uses against lesbians—weapons that can persuade us to become, in the still-apt words of the 1921 British House of Lords, "self-eradicating." What happens to our developing lesbian psyches when we cannot see accurate cultural reflections of ourselves, and how do the firewalls of propaganda enable a one-way transmission of lies?

In attempting to write a sermon for New Year's Day, I wanted to address the escalating insanity in the world, where every headline seems to portend some new Doomsday disaster. The **Sermon for a New Year** confronts the two poles that present themselves in these times: utter despair and frenetic distraction. Is there a path between these two poles that can allow us to face the new year—or new day—with courage, optimism, and purpose?

The **Sermon on Logotherapy** unearths a school of psychotherapy founded by Holocaust survivor Victor Frankl. I had never heard of this school, and I was struck by the sanity, the morality, and the practicality embedded in its tenets. So much of modern psychology appears to be causing the very syndromes it would purport to cure, that it seemed to me important to explore alternative schools of thought, and especially a therapy founded by a man who had been to the absolute depths of Western cultural depravity and who had survived and drawn conclusions from his survival.

Considerations about what constitutes mental health are recurring topics at the Lesbian Tent Revival, because lesbians face the patriarchal double whammy of being female and attempting primary intimacy with other females. We are greatly at risk of being scapegoated and gaslighted, and because of this, we can often become unwitting agents of our own oppression. The **Sermon on Toxic Self-Sufficiency** confronts one of these ways in which we become our own worst enemy.

Complex PTSD is a controversial diagnosis, and the **Sermon on Complex PTSD** explores the reasons and agendas behind this controversy. Because it is a condition that is so frequently misdiagnosed, it behooves those of us with traumatic childhood histories to understand it, and to understand the potentially fatal consequences of a misdiagnosis. Behaviors associated with Complex PTSD can be seen as natural responses to specific forms of trauma—a far cry from the "broken brain."

How can anyone fall in love with their oppressor? Stockholm Syndrome explains the dynamic, and it also provides us with possible clues for answering larger questions about entire cultures of women that appear to embrace our oppression and resist efforts for liberation. The **Sermon on Stockholm Syndrome** shifts the focus away from questions about lesbian identity and toward questions about "What is a straight woman?"

Betrayal, especially repeated betrayal, can actually alter the way in which the brain functions. I wrote the **Sermon on**

Betrayal to help us understand the effect of serial betrayals and our adaptations to them. As lesbians, we often come in for a greater share of these experiences, and I wanted to share strategies for hope and healing.

Two of my sermons, the ones on "Secrets of Salience" and on "Radical Humility," were written for that intense forever-final weekend of the Michigan Womyn's Music Festival. The **Sermon on Secrets of Salience** was written for the opening Revival of the week, and the Sermon on Radical Humility was written for that agonizing last day.

We all came to that Festival to say good-bye. How could we make the most of that precious week? Could we examine our default "salience filters" to gain an understanding of how our experiences are shaped by phobia and compulsions, habits and attitudes? Could we actually reprogram these filters to make sure that we were using this last time together to experience the things that really are the most important?

And the **Sermon on Radical Humility** was my way of ministering to our collective grief over the end of the Festival. It reaches deep beyond our third-dimensional experience of so-called reality, with a quantum leap behind the narrow apertures of our senses. One of my favorite expressions from the Festival is "I see you on the path, " because the Festival enabled so many of us to really see and be seen in a context outside the patriarchy, a radical experience for many. This sermon offers a tool—radical humility—for holding onto a deeper and more dimensional understanding of that experience.

Two years after the Festival, women began an organized effort to purchase the Land that had hosted the Michigan Womyn's Music Festival for several decades. I wrote the **Sermon on Buying the Land** from the perspective of a lesbian and feminist historian, and also as a profoundly censored playwright. It has been a survival strategy for me to research who and what gets remembered, as well as who and what gets forgotten, buried, stolen, or appropriated.

In 2017, the price of not confronting came home to me tragically in the death of a friendship that I had valued a great deal. I wrote the **Sermon on Confronting** to work through my part in this death, and also to encourage women to consider the inevitable price we pay when we choose not to confront. In a culture that does not encourage confrontation, it's small wonder so many of us—especially women—are unskilled and reluctant to stand up for ourselves, especially with those with whom we are close. The sermon explores some tools and strategies for changing behaviors and attitudes.

In 2017, we experienced the first year of a presidency that has proven to be deeply divisive. At a time when global environmental and military crises call for unprecedented levels of bipartisan cooperation and international alliances, we are becoming more and more polarized in a swamp of abusive rhetoric. I wrote the **Sermon on Holding Contradiction** to address this urgent political need, and also to explore how black-and-white thinking, or "inability to hold contradiction," is associated with trauma survivors, pre-recovery. The subject is highly charged, and this sermon goes boldy where few lesbians have gone before.

Finally, I wrote the **Sermon on Dying Well**. I wrote it, because all around me, friends and colleagues are *not* dying well. Drawing on Stephen Jenkinsen's book *Die Wise*, I invite my beloved Sisters of the Sacred Synapse to engage in some of our mightiest, most radical synapsing ever around a subject that we will all come to know intimately: our own deaths.

Sermon on Prostitution

Sisters, today I am going to be talking about prostitution.

And I know what you're thinking. You're thinking that this is the Lesbian Tent Revival and so nobody here needs a sermon on prostitution. And that's partly true, but it's also partly not true. And it's partly not true, because there are a lot of people out there—well-intentioned people—who are having difficulty synapsing fully on this subject, and there are a lot of reasons for that…mainly that we live in patriarchy and so patriarchy has an investment in prostituting women and girls, and keeping people from thinking clearly on the subject.

So, sisters, I am going to be talking about prostitution today in the hopes that we can all get super-smart on the subject of the subject. And by that I mean that when we run into these folks who are not synapsing fully, we will have a strategy and facts and a synaptic roadmap to help us build the linkages that will enable these folks to follow our arguments and connect up the dots in their own brains. And this is really important, because the conditions that enable prostitution or ignorance or denial about it are the conditions that maintain patriarchy with all of its horrors. We are our sisters keepers. Okay? So listen up!

Because it's not enough to know what we think about prostitution. And some of our lesbian sisters are out there working on the front lines… but all of us can do more. All of us have been in the presence of inadequate synapsing on this issue, and when we fail to speak up on this issue, we fail to

1

speak up for ourselves and for our planet, and that hurts our spirit. And we die a little bit. Okay… so today we're going to learn how to speak up effectively, and so after today we will all be better allies for ourselves and our sisters.

Okay… Now, I'm going to be doin' a lot of quoting today. I'm going to be doing a lot of quoting of Dr. Catharine MacKinnon. She is one fierce and mighty synapser, and the blueprints and wiring charts of her thinking can help us optimize our own brains. So… I'm going to be quoting quite a bit from her paper titled "Trafficking, Prostitution, and Inequality." And you can download that from the Internet if you want to. And you can share it.

Okay… well, first off, Sister Catharine starts out by saying that folks have all kinds of attitudes about prostitution, which we already know: Some folks support it wholeheartedly. Some think it's politically correct to tolerate it and oppose any efforts to do anything about it. And then she says that most folks assume that it's necessary or inevitable but harmless. And that's a lot of what Sister Carolyn finds in the women's community. Especially with the women who are not radical feminists. And there are lesbians who think like that, and there are women who identify sincerely as feminists who think like that. So listen up:

What it comes down to is this: Many folks believe that there is a good kind of prostitution and a bad kind. Or at least a tolerable kind (partly because they believe it's inevitable) and an intolerable kind. In other words, there is a right way to do it and a wrong way to do it. And they are against the wrong

2

way and the intolerable way, but they endorse or tolerate the right way. And this is the list that Sister Catharine has given us about these attitudes. These are really important, because these are the foundation of the strategy we're going to be working with today:

1. Adult prostitution is okay; child prostitution is not okay.
2. Indoor prostitution is okay... or at least better than, outdoor prostitution.
3. Legal prostitution is different from and better than illegal prostitution.
4. Voluntary prostitution is good; forced prostitution is bad.
5. And, finally... trafficking is always terrible, evil, and unconscionable, but prostitution is different from trafficking and can be okay, sometimes... see above.

So that's how the popular synapsing goes around the issue.

Let's review: Adult vs. child, indoor vs. outdoor, legal vs. illegal, voluntary vs. involuntary, prostitution vs. trafficking. The reason I went over this is because this is the strategy. This is the way we lay out the synaptic campaign. When we are in the presence of folks who are talking about prostitution like it's a good thing, or a necessary and inevitable thing... the first thing we do is get them to clarify what kind of prostitution they talking about... Surely not prostitution of chidren...? Surely not trafficking? We get them to articulate exactly what they are defining as the good or tolerable forms of prostitution. This will show us where the holes in their thinking are.

Because, sisters, these neat little divisions of "good-and-bad" or "better-or-worse" only exist in the minds of those whose understanding of prostitution and the way it works is synaptically inadequate. These dichotomies are not supported by the facts. Why do so many folks hold onto theory and beliefs so utterly unsupported by reality? Because of who mediates our perceptions of reality and why. I mean, think about *Pretty Woman* with Julia Roberts, and how iconic that movie became. The prostituted woman who ends up marrying her wealthy and wonderful john. Contrast that with a film about a real prostituted woman, like Eileen Wuornos, who ended up murdering the men who made the mistake of assuming that they could perpetrate any kind of abuse on her because she was prostituted. What's the title of her film? "*Monster.*" And, it's not coincidental that Wuornos was a lesbian. Well... don't get me started. But people synapse inadequately about prostitution in part because of these cultural misrepresentations. It would be nice if we were all Hollywood moguls, but we are not, so we will need to do our work on the ground, changing one mind at a time.

Okay, let's start with the adult-versus-child thing. Well, what we know today is that the majority of prostituted women entered prostitution when they were young... children, in fact, and that this age of entry appears to be dropping. Sister Catharine goes on to say that the majority of prostituted women and girls she met in India were first prostituted at the age of ten. In a study of 200 women presently and formerly

4

prostituted in San Francisco, 78% began as minors, with 62% being under sixteen. So… if child prostitution is bad, but adult prostitution is okay, does that mean that it's suddenly okay when the girl who was prostituted at ten has her eighteenth birthday? If what she experienced the day before her birthday was an atrocity, and the same experience the day after is an empowering career choice, what exactly is it about the magic birthday that has made the difference? And, since she did not grow up with any kind of understanding of the atrocity being perpetrated on her, how informed can this empowering adult career choice be?

Yeah, that word. "Choice." Another thing we know about prostitution is that prostituted women were and are often survivors of child sexual abuse. There have been a number of studies, and of course Sister Catharine cites a bunch of them. The percentages range between 65% and 95%. And, of course, these percentages have to be taken with a grain of salt, because of patterns of denial and minimization that are common with ongoing traumatization. Not to mention amnesia. So it's probable that the numbers are higher than reported. The traumatization, of course, being the ongoing prostitution. And we're going to talk about trauma later… But if a child is taught that her job, her role, her duty, her fate, her destiny, her job in the family, her identity in life is servicing adult men sexually… wouldn't that amount to torture and brainwashing, and so how does that affect this notion of "choice" that is so indispensible to that neat dichotomy between adult prostitution as "sort of okay" and child prostitution as absolutely wrong?

And if child prostitution is not okay, then where does one fit young adult prostituted women who advertise themselves and are advertised as children still, for the sake of pornography and prostitution. What does that say about the "okay-ness" of the entire genre called "barely legal?"

But let's move along. Indoor versus outdoor. Some folks feel that indoor is okay, because aren't the call girls and escort services the upper middle-class manifestation of prostitution? And isn't upper-middle-class everything always better, even in prostitution? Everybody knows that street prostitution is the bottom tier socially. I mean, isn't it better to give a blow job in an upscale brothel or at the Ritz Carleton penthouse suite, than in the drafty front seat of a beat-up car? Isn't it better to service a rich man in a luxurious environment than a poor man on a crime-ridden street? I mean wouldn't this just be common sense? No, actually it's not. Because this isn't really about employment. It's about predation; it's about *negotiated abuse*. The street prostitute may not have a lot of choice over johns, but the indoor prostitute has none at all. She is sent to a hotel, or the john arrives at her establishment and chooses her. She's basically trapped. And the street prostitute usually consummates the transaction at some indoor place anyway, making the distinction even less clear.

And is it true that the upper-middle-class john is safer than the working-class john? Actually no, it's not. The upper-middle-class john may feel greater contempt for the woman from a poverty-class background. He may feel more entitled to perform whatever acts he wants—contracted for or not— because of this power difference. He may feel he has some

6

kind of immunity from arrest in a ritzy hotel, and he may be right about that. In an environment where he has all the control, he may also feel safer not compensating the prostituted woman. So, in short, no, it's not safe to assume that johns with class privilege are going to be safer... or even more lucrative. Recently, a bunch of secret service men accompanied the President to Brazil. They procured the services of prostituted women there, promising them $800 and then refused to pay. The men traveling with the President of the United States. Yeah. Keepin' it classy.

Well, what about those brothels, especially in countries where prostitution is legal, where there have been efforts made on behalf of safety? Well, these can have features like "duress buttons"... ideally three to a room, so that the woman can reach one from a variety of different locations. Some of them have room surveillance videos. The pimps who are responsible for the security of the brothel have an added perk in that these security cameras provide a stream of pornographic activity. There is, of course, no guarantee that any filmed sexual activity will not be sold as pornography. There may be front-desk reception, where such precautions could be taken as asking the johns to leave their belts and neckties. And... some of the safer venues even have cordless lamps and other appliances. Seriously, how many of us go to our daily workplace and scan for the presence of electrical cords, out of a concern that our most valued customers, seeing cords, might be tempted to strangle us, tie us up, and/ or beat us with them? Seriously. How many of us need to have the folks in our workplace remove their belts and ties in order for us to conduct business with them without fearing strangulation?

Sisters, these are not normal employment safety conditions. Why? Because this is NOT a normal job. It's negotiated abuse. I'm going to say that again. It's negotiated abuse. It's paid rape.

What I am saying is that, in spite of all the barrels of propaganda on this issue, the prostitution of women is not a normal line of work and the brothels are not normal places of business. What is being described with these brothels are attempts to control assault, because, for so many so-called customers, it is precisely the right to assault for which they believe they have contracted. Sisters, that does *not* constitute normal working conditions.

As Sister Catharine points out, indoor often just means more pimp control and less accountability. Really, the whole indoor/outdoor thing comes down to illusion. Sister Catharine notes that when people cannot see the prostituted women, because they are working indoors, they can often imagine that they have upper-class options... that is to say, they are exercising free will, being well-paid, enjoying themselves, are relatively safe, can leave if they want to, and are not being compelled or hurt... or maybe not really all that much. None of this is true.

So now, if we are really synapsing fully, we have obliterated the imaginary clear division between adult and child prostitution and indoor versus outdoor. So now, let's move on.

What's next?

Legal versus illegal. Many folks believe that legalizing prostitution eliminates the social stigma and allows for government protections to be put into place. They believe that, where prostitution is illegal, the criminal nature of the industry is responsible for the harms that occur. Is this true? No, actually, it's not. Why? Because prostitution is not a normal job.

The stigma on prostituted women does not stem from the criminal status of prostitution. It stems from the nature of the work... which is about strange men buying access to one's body for the purpose of getting themselves off. That stigma is never going to go away, because most folks who seriously envision themselves in that situation are filled with fear, horror, or disgust—or all of the above. In fact, the folks who valorize prostitution are often incapable of imagining themselves in that situation... and they valorize it as a function of exoticizing or dehumanizing people with different racial, socio-economic, ethnic, or national background. And, of course, gender. Their so-called "alliance" is predicated on their understanding of the utter impossibility of their ever being prostituted. What kind of ally is that?

For starts, and this is just for starts, everyone agrees that trafficking is a bad thing. That's the kidnapping, drugging, hostage-taking, brainwashing, terrorizing, captivity/slavery thing, where women or girls are sold or tricked or terrorized...

Well, legalizing prostitution actually incentivizes trafficking, because all the traffickers have to do is get the women over the border to a country where prostitution is legal, and then they are home free. This has been documented in the Netherlands, Germany, Victoria in Australia, and elsewhere.

Also, illegal prostitution explodes in countries that legalize it. That seems strange, doesn't it...? But think about it: Where prostitution is legal, and where the authorities are trying to implement "harm-reduction" measures (note, not "harm elimination," but "harm *reduction*"), there are things that violent misogynists may not like... for instance, having to wear condoms, having to check their neckties and belts at the door, etc. This generates a market for prostitution that does not attempt to "harm-reduce." Johns want to go where they don't have to wear condoms, and so on. The whole point of prostitution is that men get to make women do exactly what they, the men, order them to do. Restrictions and regulations on prostitution are kind of oxymoronic. The implementation of these regulations in legal prostitution raises the price of harm-enhanced prostitution... in other words, illegal prostitution.

And then there are well-intentioned, naïve folks who believe that the solution is to legalize AND unionize. Because they have fallen for the propaganda that this is a normal job. So let's imagine union bargaining over a labor contract for prostituted women. This would have to include details about what kind of sex. As Sister Catharine says, "Suppose how much and what kind of sex was bargained over and put in a labor contract. Could it be enforced?" Seriously... And she asks us to think about the union organizer who is collecting money from the women and girls. Wouldn't that be, by definition, a pimp? Seriously, is being in a union going to do anything for the PTSD suffered by women in prostitution? Is a union going to help them leave? Did you know that 89% of women in prostitution, when asked what they need most, reply that they need to leave? This is not a normal job. I can't say that enough. This is not normal work. A normal union is not set up to help folks leave the line of work represented by the union.

Again, what we see with liberals is sloppy synapsing. They are adopting and applying theoretical models that uphold their liberal ideals, but prostitution, because it is an abuse not a job, simply does not fit the categories. And because only a tiny, tiny percentage of prostituted women—nearly all from the West—are spokespeople for legalizing prostitution, these liberals can get away with it. The 89% desperate to escape are not being heard. They are too scared, too marginalized, too drugged, or too dissociated to be on a national soapbox. And the prostituted woman who is being arrested frequently, sometimes raped by the police, may be a persuasive spokeswoman for the legalization of prostitution. She is focused on survival, and her position is understandable, but the point is not to decriminalize prostitution, but to decriminalize the women who are coerced or forced to sell their bodies by poverty, by terrorism, by childhood trauma, or by lack of opportunity.

And there is a country that has decriminalized the women. It's Sweden, and it's very interesting what is happening there. Here is Sister Catharine MacKinnon on the subject: "What Sweden has done is to situate prostitution in the context of violence against women and strongly criminalize the buyers accordingly, making purchasing sex a crime, and enforced it,

11

together with extending some help (if not enough) to those who want to leave. Against his demand to buy her for sex, this law says she is not for sale, or rent."

Yes, they had to train the police. They had to change the notion that prostitution is about evil, predatory, disease-ridden women tempting and exploiting and infecting good men who could not withstand their powers of seduction. They had to teach the police that it is the buyers who are the exploiters. So now the police in Sweden surveil and arrest the men. Does it work? Yes, actually it does. Arresting the women has never worked. Why? Because the women are desperate. It's like arresting people for trying to feed their children. Not going to work. But arresting the men works. Street prostitution in Sweden is down by half, and Sweden has the lowest trafficking rate in Europe.

Okay. So much for legal versus illegal.

Now let's talk about the voluntary versus involuntary. We've already touched on the problematic notion of "choice" when child sexual abuse and/ or child prostitution has been present. But let's really look at this issue of volition.

I'm going to cite Dr. Mimi Silbert now. Who is she? Mimi Silbert is the Board Chair, President, and CEO of the Delancey Street Foundation, which has been called "The best and most successful rehabilitation program in the world". Delancey Street serves ex-felons, prostitutes, substance abusers, and others who have hit bottom, in six national centers. So Dr. Silbert not only knows prostituted women, but she understands what they need when they get out.

Dr. Mimi Silbert, in her work, has come to an interesting conclusion. Her conclusion is that prostituted women are "the most raped class of women in history." *"The most raped class of women in history."* And this has everything to do with their "job." You know, that "job" that liberals are so fond of framing as an empowered career... although not one that they would ever consider for themselves.

Studies of varying sample sizes and methodologies in diverse locations found 40% to 85% of women reported being raped in prostitution. Now Sister Catharine has extensively documented the harm. I'm just going to skim through her footnotes here... Y'all can look them up.

- One study found 40% were raped in prostitution, and about half of those were raped more than five times.
- Another study found victims said they were raped nearly once a week.
- Another study found 75% said they were raped by the johns, 62% on the streets in other contexts, and 43% by men identifying themselves as police.
- Another study: 70% by clients, an average of 31.3 times *apiece.*
- Another study found that, in addition to being raped in prostitution, half were beaten once a month or more.

The point is, this is not a normal job, a normal career, a normal industry. It is a human rights abuse. And at this point it might be helpful to look at exactly what the women are selling. Supposedly it's sex. But what does that mean? Well, looking up sex is an interesting thing. Because the definition for sex keeps using words like "sexual." Seems that the dictionary makers can't seem to define it without resorting to self-referential terms. Which is like saying, "dog" is a "doglike" animal.

When it comes to sex it seems the lexicographers break their own rules. Why? Why would they do that? Because to define sex along, say, radical feminist lines, would be to make it clear it is NOT something that could ever be bought or sold or coerced or forced. Because a lesbian feminist definition of sex would make it clear that the men who are buying the bodies of women are NOT buying sex. They are abusing.

Sisters, we know how important words are. We know that Sister Toni Cade Bambara referred to "acts of language." Not being able to define sex in terms of the SUBJECT, sisters, that is a huge synaptic gap, a vast hole in the web through which millions of women and girls fall every year. Not being able to think clearly about sex, not being able to define it accurately in ways that insist on personal ownership of sexuality are important in patriarchy. It means there will be confusion over prostitution, confusion over whether or not sex is a saleable commodity.

Well, let's take a minute to consider what we might use instead of "sex." This is one of those Tent Revival digressions.

14

And, sisters, a lesbian digression, is more often than not, going to be the main event. Can I get a witness?

And, by the way, even the dictionary tells us that "sex" has a bullshit definition... In the *Merriam-Webster Dictionary,* sex is defined as "sexually motivated phenomena or behavior." Not too helpful. Kind of like looking up "tennis" and reading that it is a "tennis phenomenon or behavior." Looking up "sexual" is not much help either: "having or involving sex"... which of course leads us back to "sexual."

So, sisters, let us commit one of Toni Cade Bambara's "acts of language." Let's creat a gynocentric, subjective word, referencing the clitoris not the vagina.

Here's an idea... What about the words "cypriate" and "cypriation" for female genital activity initiated by the subject, for the primary intention of experiencing a pleasurable arousal of the clitoris? For example, "Last night, next to the waterfall, I cypriated with my partner." Or... "Cypriation at the full moon can be especially intense."

I admit I am taking my cue from the late, great Monique Wittig, whose acts of language opened my eyes to wild possibility. In her Lesbian Peoples: Material for a Dictionary, she and Sande Zeig coined the word "la cyprine" to refer to the vaginal secretions that signal sexual desire. *"Sécrétion vaginale, signe physique du désir sexuel. Une agitation trouble l'écoulement de la cyprine."* That's Monique's French for "Vaginal secretion, physical sign of sexual desire. Agitation disturbs the flow of the cyprine."

15

Where did she get "cyprine?" From the island of Cyprus, the legendary birthplace of Aphrodite, the goddess of love.

Obviously cypriation does not refer to many of the acts that are considered sex or sexual in the heteropatriarchal world. In fact, it probably refers to only a tiny minority. But adopting the use of this word will require that the subject own her agency, and it will also validate her own pleasure as something of primary, defining significance.

Sisters, there should never have been one word that could be used to refer to pleasurable, welcome sexual activity for women and, at the same time, any and all violations or torture of her genitals. There should never have been a word for sexual activity that confused an act designed for procreation with an act designed for a woman's pleasure. There should never be a word that can be taken to assume that actions pleasing to men and their genitals are or should be pleasing to women and our genitals. Sex and rape are only synonymous for rapists. Oh, and by the way, "vagina" and "vulva" are only synonymous where the clit and the woman's pleasure are incidental or irrelevant. Think about it.

What has happened is that women's experience and women's anatomy and women's pleasure have been stolen in a linguistic equivalent of three-card monte. Sisters, take back the clit! Occupy the dictionary!

End of digression.

Let's get back to the trauma… the beatings, the rapes that are the so-called occupation hazard of this so-called line of work. Here's something Sister Catharine shares with us: "…women's measured level of post-traumatic stress ("PTSD") is equivalent to that of combat veterans or victims of torture or raped women. PTSD results from going through atrocities you cannot mentally sustain. It often accompanies dissociation: you put the violation away, leave mentally, repress or deny it or act like it is not there inside you, disappear the self who knows it happened to get through the day. Often women in prostitution are addicted to drugs; many use substantial amounts of alcohol, too, as a result of what they are going through. Sometimes the drugs are pushed on them by pimps to addict them."

Not a normal job. "Combat veterans or victims of torture or rape." People with *enemies*. That's an odd way to describe customer relations. But not an odd way to describe abuse.

We are talking about the notion that voluntary prostitution is good, but involuntary is bad. Well, who in their right mind would choose a "job" with such deadly hazards? Does any loving parent raise their daughters to dream of becoming prostitutes?

Just who is it who is "choosing" prostitution? As Sister Catharine notes, "Everywhere, prostituted people are overwhelmingly poor, indeed normally destitute. There is no disagreement on this fact." I'm going to repeat that. "There is no disagreement on that…" even by the liberals who support the idea that prostitution can be voluntary and empowering.

They do not disagree that these women are poor and often desperate. The most frequent reason given by people in prostitution is urgent financial need. Urgent, as in food, shelter. Urgent. And, Sister Catharine goes on to note, almost nobody gets out of poverty through prostituting. So much for "career." In fact, as she further notes, they are lucky to get out with their lives, given mortality rates. AND… many prostituted women find themselves deeper and deeper in debt, as pimps charge rents and take percentages. And then, too, there is the drug or alcohol addiction. Often the pimp is also the supplier of the illegal drugs.

So, if one believes in voluntary prostitution, let it be noted that the majority of women choosing prostitution of their own free will are in situations of desperate poverty. Seems to be some kind of synaptic disconnect in that statement, no?

The women "choosing" prostitution are also disproportionately members of socially disadvantaged racial groups or lower castes. For example, there are a disproportionately high number of Native women prostituted in Vancouver, BC. This would suggest, in the words of Sister Catharine, "that who is in prostitution often derives from colonialism and persists after it. No one chooses to be born into poverty… No one chooses the racial group or caste one is born into. No country freely chooses to be colonized or the post-colonial social pathologies that so often organize this industry… These circumstances are not chosen by any of them."

And yet, the liberals tell us, these women "choose" prostitution.

We have already touched on the third non-choice element that pre-determines who "chooses" to prostitute themselves: Childhood. We know that a large percentage, if not the majority, of women in prostitution were sexually abused and/or prostituted as children. Children cannot choose who they want to live with, where they want to live. They usually cannot protect themselves from assault by adults. What they can choose to do is dissociate. They can choose to take drugs or drink to manage the pain of their victimhood. They can learn to eroticize anxiety, to identify with the perpetrator, because these mental tricks can generate an illusion of control, and an illusion of control in the absence of any real control, can save a life.

Unfortunately, these survival strategies cobbled together out of the limited skill set and resources of a child, will often persist into adulthood. This same substance abuse, dissociation, amnesia, eroticizing of anxiety, or identity with the perpetrator may inform the so-called voluntary choice to prostitute oneself.

Okay... poverty, socially disadvantaged background, child abuse. These make a mockery out of "choice," and unmask the colonialism, capitalism, and adultism behind these notions of choice... So, sisters, this is how we do it, one attitude at a time.

So, say, you're in a conversation about prostitution, and folks are expressing support or qualified support of the institution. You jump right in and clarify... You say something like this: "Okay, hold on a minute, now I'm a little confused. You're talking about ADULT and VOLUNTARY prostitution, right... and ideally, INDOORS and LEGAL... right?" And they will probably agree.

Then you say, "Okay, but now I'm even more confused, because it's my understanding that those distinctions can't really be made in the real world. Maybe you can help me with that. This is what I understand about the "adult" category..."

And then of course, you hit the points that Sister Catharine MacKinnon has so brilliantly made and that Sister Carolyn has so evangelically reiterated. And you just go right on down that line: adult, voluntary, indoors, legal. Bam bam bam bam.

I recommend you end with legal, because then you can wind up with Sweden. And it is my belief that Sweden has got the right approach. It's called the "Nordic model." Women can and will sell whatever they have to in order to survive. It is the MEN who exploit them who are the criminals. It is the men who are exercising free will and choice.

All right. So you all go out there and preach it, because there is a tower of ignorance and a continent of slavery on this issue. We got our work cut out.

Blessed be.

Sermon on Stories

Sisters, today we are going to consider stories. Stories are great things. Stories can be maps. They can be templates. They can be guidebooks. They can be cautionary tales. They can be mirrors. They can be latitude and longitude. They can be spiritual vitamins. They can be precious heritage. Lesbian poet Muriel Rukeyser said, "The universe is made of stories, not atoms." That sounds kind of poetic until you look hard at what we call reality, at quantum physics. Then it's actually pretty scientific. And here's poet Maya Angelou: "There is no greater agony than bearing an untold story inside you." Which brings me back to that great quotation from the Gospel of St. Thomas, "If you bring forth what is within you, what you bring forth will save you. If you do not bring forth what is within you, what you do not bring forth will destroy you."

Now you can bring forth that "thing that is in you" in poetry, or painting, or dance, or theatre, or music, or story. And if you bring it forth as story, it may be a story that only you can interpret, and that's okay.

But stories can also be propaganda. That's why we're going to synapse around the whole thing of "story" today. Because the propaganda stories can get us thinking along lines that will cause us to betray our own best interests… and often, in scrubbing off the layers of falsehood in popular myths, like fairy tales or folklore or patriotic myths, we can recognize some life-saving truths that underlie the distortion or the appropriation. Kinda like when you find a masterpiece underneath that painting of dogs playing cards.

So that's what we're doing today.

We're going to look at a very popular story in the colonization of America. We're going to look at the story of Sacagawea. Most of us will remember that she was the Native American woman who accompanied the Lewis and Clark expedition in their efforts to locate a route across the western half of the continent, to the Pacific Ocean. She's a big heroine in American history, and her image—or some artist's idea of her image—is on a dollar coin, and she's been on a postage stamp, and folks love to tell the traditional story about her, because it's about a strong woman on a bold adventure, and it's also about interracial harmony.

Now, sisters, those aren't bad reasons for telling stories... except that in the case of Sacagawea, they aren't the whole truth. And the parts of the truth that they are hiding are really, really important parts of the story. And there is also a story underneath that is not being told.

So, let's get out those tools for scraping off those layers of cultural whitewash and mansplainery, and see a little bit more of what's really going on in this story.

Sacagawea was born into the Shoshone tribe in Idaho around 1788, and when she was eleven or twelve years old, she was in a Shoshone hunting camp that was attacked by the Hidatsa, a Siouan tribe of Native Americans. In this raid, four Shoshone men and four Shoshone women, and several boys were killed. Sacagawea was taken captive and enslaved. Remember, she's eleven or twelve years old. And these Hidatsa force her to walk with them back to where they live in North Dakota, which is about a thousand miles away. So here's this eleven or twelve-year-old child who has survived a massacre of family and friends, and she's now enslaved, and she's having to march for a thousand miles back into North Dakota from Montana, and when she gets there, she is—you know—she's still an enslaved child.

And then, one night, there is this French trapper who shows up in the village, and he plays some kind of gambling game with the Hidatsa, and he wins. And to pay off their debt, the Hidatsa give him Sacagawea. Who is twelve by now, or possibly thirteen. So now she's his slave. He already has bought another Shoshone captive girl, "Otter Woman," from the Hidatsa. He calls these enslaved children his "wives." It is a formalized child-rape arrangement brokered by adults. And, sisters, remember, every single time you read or hear something about Sacagawea's French trapper husband and you do not raise hell, you are actually participating in legitimizing this child-rape arrangement. He was her owner, her captor, and her rapist. Period.

Sacagawea conceived around the age of fourteen, and the reason we know this is because she was pregnant in the winter of 1804-5, when Lewis and Clark showed up in the Hidatsa village and started negotiating with Sacagawea's perpetrator for his services as a guide. Lewis and Clark were the two men leading this expedition commissioned by the US government.

They were leading twenty-nine white men and one African American man, who was enslaved. Sacagawea's perpetrator told Lewis and Clark that the pregnant child was his wife, and he negotiated a fee for her services as a Shoshone translator—a fee that would be paid to him, of course. As her captor's so-called wife, Sacagawea never received a dime for her services—or any form of compensation—for the work that she did.

So here we are, with this fourteen-year-old, pregnant girl, in the company of thirty-two men, most of whom speak a language she can't understand. She is the only Native American among them, and the only female. She gave birth en route, and, according to Lewis, who attended the birth, it was a very painful and violent delivery. Afterwards, she became desperately ill with what, from Lewis' journal notes, appears to have been a severe pelvic inflammatory infection, possibly due to her enslaver's continual postpartum rape of her. In his journal, Lewis expressed a suspicion that she was a victim of a transmitted venereal disease. She came very close to dying, but she managed to recover. She spent the rest of the trip with her baby strapped to her back.

Sacagawea trekked on this expedition for two years, four months, and ten days. Sisters, she walked *eight thousand miles* with these white men and the African American enslaved man… with a baby on her back. She forded rivers and climbed steep mountains and crossed deserts and swamps in snow and rain and sweltering sun. She translated for the men, she foraged for them, she cooked for them, and she did the sewing, mending, and cleaning of their clothes… you know, the "women's work."

There have been whitewashing and mansplaining efforts to downplay her work as a guide, but the truth is, she was responsible for pointing out the pass they should take through the Rockies and the pass they should take into the Yellowstone basin… the Bozeman Pass. Kind of a big deal, locating these passes.

Oh, and by the way, the only reason we have the record of this expedition is because Sacagawea had the foresight and agility to rescue Lewis's journals when they were tumbling out of a capsized boat. For her pains, she had a river named after her. But no pay.

One of the greatest services that Sacagawea provided was protection. By this time, Native American tribes had come to assume, and assume rightly, that any group of white men traveling into their territory probably constituted some kind of war party. They had learned that it was better to attack first and then try to figure out who they were later. But the fact that this group included a Native American woman with a baby was taken as evidence that these men came in peace. In other words, Sacagawea saved all their lives and probably many times over.

So, eventually, the expedition gets to the western part of Oregon, to the coast. And they set up a camp and start sending parties down to the beach to see the actual ocean. And these parties are reporting that some kind of "great fish" has washed up on the beach—possibly a whale. And, unbelievably, these men were not going to allow Sacagawea to leave the camp to go see it. Unbelievable. She had to beg and plead with them, and this was so unusual on her part, that Lewis wrote about it in his journal. And it really pisses me off that she did all this enormous work, *as a child, with a newborn, involuntarily,* and then when they finally reach their goal—the Pacific Ocean—where there's this magical, giant fish, this eighth wonder of the world, they make Sacagawea beg and plead just to be able to see it. If there is ever any historical doubt about her degree of autonomy on this expedition, that should lay it to rest finally and forever. She had none.

Sacagawea was dead by the age of twenty-five. Still with her rapist/captor, she was living at a fur trading post in Montana at the time of her death. She was very sick and wanted to go home to her people. She reportedly died of typhus, a disease transmitted by a human body louse—a disease associated with conditions of poor hygiene and sanitation. But, if Lewis was correct in suspecting that Sacagawea had been infected with a venereal disease by her rapist, she may have died from a fever associated with that. We know that she left behind an infant girl, and the typhus or the venereal disease may have taken hold during postpartum weakness. The daughter appears not to have survived. The son was taken in by Meriwether Lewis, who paid for his schooling.

I know. It's a horrible story, isn't it? Sacagawea was obviously heroically strong, but she was a victim throughout her short life. From age eleven, she was separated from her people and enslaved. She was a victim of ongoing rape from puberty and subjected to involuntary pregnancies.

It's a story of endurance, but it's not the story of multi-cultural diversity in the early years of the US. Sacagawea is not the poster woman for biracial marriage. She was obviously powerful, but she was not empowered. If there is any multi-cultural story to be told here, it is a shameful story of the collusion of powerful men—French, Hidatsa, and Anglo American—in the exploitation of an enslaved, female child. It's a disgusting tale of adult males bonding through the bartering for forced labor and victimization of a Shoshone girl. However divergent their cultures, these men were all in agreement in their misogyny. They all colluded in characterizing the formalized child-rape arrangement as a legalized marriage.

But, sisters, there is another story… one that is very important. It's actually found between the lines in Lewis' journal. Let's take a look… Bear with me, because we're going to have to backtrack a little bit in the story before we get to it…

So at one point in their travels, the expedition ended up camping at the very place where Sacagawea was captured and abducted by the Hidatsa as a little girl. This was the place where she lost her tribe, her family, her history, her culture, her freedom... and, sadly, her childhood. This was the place from which she was forced to undertake a journey of a thousand miles with her enemy.

So, when the Lewis and Clark Expedition arrived at this former Shoshone hunting camp, Sacagawea told them the story of the massacre and here is what Lewis wrote in his journal: "I cannot discover that she shews any immotion of sorrow in recollecting this event, or of joy in being again restored to her native country; if she has enough to eat and a few trinkets to wear I believe she would be perfectly content anywhere."

He seems to be describing her as someone who is kind of shallow or emotionally under-developed... "primitive" in the sense of being in some early stage of evolution or history. He appears to be comparing her affect to that which he believes he might experience, had he been in her shoes... which is as ridiculous as it is unfair. As a white, male colonizer, he has absolutely no context for understanding the trauma of her past, or the context of her ongoing rape and enslavement. He does not appear to understand that he is complicit in enabling her ongoing enslavement.

Sisters, it sounds to me like Sacagawea was experiencing very severe post-traumatic stress syndromes. She sounds numb, possibly experiencing dissociation from her situation, or maybe even depersonalization... which is a post-traumatic syndrome where your own thoughts and feelings seem unreal, or like they don't belong to you. Depersonalization is a kind of complete loss of identity, which makes sense when you consider that her trauma was far from over. And when we consider that this is what Lewis wrote in his journal, it's a description of Sacagawea that lets him off the hook. Since she doesn't seem to register any kind of emotional response to this terrible massacre and abduction… he doesn't have to feel bad about not paying her, or pretending she's a married woman, when he knows damn well she's a slave. It's kind of convenient for him to see her as someone who doesn't feel any pain… It's like the way they tell you that lobsters don't feel it when you drop them in the boiling water. What they mean is *we* don't have to feel it.

This part of the story tells a sad truth about much of human nature. We are incentivized to see and hear what will benefit us. That is a fact. Which is why we, at the Tent Revival, spend such an inordinate amount of time working to reprogram our brains so that we can make a primary commitment to the truth. We do that reprogramming by learning to incentivize ourselves against the grain of a culture that will punish us for knowing or speaking the truth. We do this because any time the truth is not a primary commitment, we are greatly at risk of not seeing it, of deluding ourselves… because, sisters, this is patriarchy, and knowing the truth, our truth, women's truth… well, that can get you killed.

But let's get back to the truth about Sacagawea, who is most often depicted as a grown woman making her own choices about helping these heroic white pathfinders, blazing a trail that will "civilize" the West… We, as a nation, are not much incentivized to adjust that soft-focus lens to bring into sharp definition the fourteen-year-old slave child on a mission that will spell defeat for her people. And one of the reasons why we love that grown-woman-in-charge-of-her-own-life narrative is because it tells us she is choosing—sisters, *choosing*—to help men. There are no other women anywhere in sight for most of those eight thousand miles. A Native woman *choosing* to help the white men... *and* even though she has a baby, she takes total, complete responsibility for him. Straps that baby on her back and never skips a beat while she does all the domestic work of caring for these thirty-three grown-ass men. And then she turns her paycheck over to her "husband!" What a fine example. Look at what she did! Now, surely women today, with all the conveniences of modern civilization, can take those three days of maternity leave and turn their kid over to day care and get right back to work. Be like Sacagawea! Don't be thinking of motherhood as a second job or a sacred responsibility! Don't be missing your women friends! Don't be hoarding that paycheck! Don't be complaining and comparing! Do it all and don't take any credit for it! Be like Sacagawea!

Story, sisters. Story is everything. It's the web of synapses we weave to make meaning. As astrologist Caroline Casey says, "Imagination lays the track for the reality train." It surely does, sisters. And a story is like a line on a railroad... like the Long Island Rail Road, or the Metro-North Railroad, or the Staten Island Railway. The story is a route with a destination. We take these stories in when we hear them. We pass them along. We put them in our toolkits for how to live our lives. Story is everything. We have to think critically about the stories we are given. Who is doing the giving and for what purpose? Who is going to benefit from them? We have never had so many stories. Not just books... but Hulu and Netflix and Youtube and cable and movies and podcasts. So many stories... But how many of them tell our truths? Women's truths? Lesbian truths?

African American author and activist Toni Cade Bambara wrote an essay titled, "The Issue is Salvation," and in it she says, "I work to produce stories that save our lives." That's what we should all be doing. And if we can't write them, then we can go into uncovering the truth about the ones they hand us.

And that's exactly what we are going to do now. We are going to go digging for that story that is hidden between the lines of Lewis' journal. And keep in mind that Meriwether Lewis' journal... the one that Sacagawea dove into the water to rescue, is five thousand pages long. That's a lot of pages. But the part that we are are digging for is just two sentences. Two sentences out of five thousand pages. Kind of like a needle in a haystack. But, sisters, if you know what you are needing to hear, if you have a pretty good idea of what these patriarchs are trying to hide... you can find that needle. It's going to be like a magnetized needle... a compass needle, pointing us to the truth.

So here they are... Here are those precious sentences from Meriwether Lewis' journal... the needle in the haystack... This was on August 15, 1805. Lewis is talking about when the expedition came to the camp where Sacagawea's people lived... where her tribe was—her family—before that massacre and abduction when she was eleven. And keep in mind, she's been enslaved this whole time. She's never been back to her people. This is the first time she's seeing them in four years.

"We soon drew near to the [Shoshone] camp, and just as we approached it a woman made her way through the crowd towards Sacagawea, and recognizing each other, they embraced with the most tender affection. The meeting of these two young women had in it something peculiarly touching, not only in the ardent manner in which their feelings were expressed, but from the real interest of their situation..."

I like that Meriwether Lewis is noticing the "real interest of their situation." And I like that, after describing Sacagawea as pretty emotionless and shallow, he is now going back on that completely and describing a scene that is ardent... which means passionate, and tender, touching and overflowing with affection. Obviously, Sacagawea had been keeping her emotional life sacred... for another female and a woman of her tribe.

So who is this other fifteen-year-old Shoshone girl who is embracing Sacagawea so ardently? Well, her name was Pop-pank. She and Sacagawea grew up together, and they were at that hunting camp together when the massacre happened and Sacagawea was taken prisoner. Pop-pank had jumped into the river and, leaping like a fish, had managed to get to the other side and escape capture.

And here she was when the Lewis and Clark expedition showed up to try to buy some horses on their way to the Pacific. And here she was seeing again her beloved girlhood friend, Sacagawea... now with a baby and enslaved. And this is what Lewis recorded: the reunion of these two girls—and they were both still girls—embracing each other, tender and passionate at the same time.

We can hold onto that story as tightly as Sacagawea held onto Pop-pank. It is a story of an authenticity that resists colonization, of a memory that resists the distortions and erasures of trauma, of a bond that defies appropriation in the colonial narrative.

Let us not be fooled by the fact it only warrants two sentences in the journal of Lewis, or that it was only a few stationary minutes out of a journey of hundreds of days and thousands of miles. It is a glimpse into reality, into eternity. It shows up the colonial, patriarchal, misogynist pageant for what it is: an utter sham.

I think of something that 19th century feminist author Charlotte Perkins Gilman said... She said, "Eternity is not something that begins after you are dead. It is going on all the time." And every now and then we can part the curtain and catch that glimpse. Maybe only a glimpse, but it contains all that we need.

Sisters, let us hold close those two sentences that Meriwether Lewis wrote, not understanding even as he wrote them, because they illuminate the pages of history more than all the rest of the words in his journal.

Take this story, sisters, and shine the light of it into your own aching lesbian heart. Blessed be!

Sermon on Jealousy

All right, now, sisters. We all know about the F word—feminism. And we all know about the L-word—lesbian… but today we're gonna talk about the J-word. That's right. The J-word. Now the reason why folks refer to certain words with just a letter is because they're afraid to say them. They're afraid to say "feminist," because that might upset some folks. Folks of the male persuasion, mostly. They're afraid to say "lesbian" because that might upset even more folks. So they kind of dance around it with F-word and L-word.

But of course, the reason they dance around them is that these words are powerful, and it's a powerful thing to claim them. You *invoke* words like "feminist" and "lesbian," because you can't say the word without calling up all the ancestors who were feminists and lesbians, and all the hard-won truths they purchased with their lives. These are not words to be messed around with. So when you see folks doing that coy "F-word," "L-word" thing, understand that they are aware that it is too dangerous for them to invoke those words, because of the powerful synapsing that might result… and they are afraid they cannot handle it. They are afraid they will look like Mickey Mouse being the sorceror's apprentice. That's a reference to the film *Fantasia* for you younger sisters. And that fear comes from not having one's tribe yet. But if you are at the Lesbian Tent Revival, you have found your tribe, so let's invoke, sisters!

Feminism! Lesbian!

And then lets put them together and watch the fire just shoot out of our brains: Lesbian-feminism!

You know I always say, "That's not a hyphen between lesbian and feminism... It's a *weld*!" The weld makes things even stronger than they were before the break.

All right. But today we're going to talk about the J-Word.

Jealousy. That's the J-word. Why am I referring to it with a letter? Because it's a scary word. It's a word that I seldom hear in lesbian communities. It's like we're all afraid to admit that lesbians can be jealous. Like something is going to explode or fall apart or be permanently ruptured if we say that word.

And before someone jumps in to ask if I'm talking about envy or jealousy... I will clarify: Envy is when you want something that someone else has. Jealousy is when you feel resentment over what that other person has, because in your mind you are more entitled to it.

Well... okay, then. The J-Word. I'm going to say it today, so we'll just see.

Now, given how much we lesbians love naming oppressions, why do we have so much difficulty admitting that we do oppress each other with jealousy?

I think it's because, if we admit to jealousy, we might have to admit to the causes of jealousy. It's an inconvenient truth that some of us have more than others: more brains, more health, more money, more formal education, more physical ability, more youth, more experience, and so on. Inequality is real and all the most heartfelt yearning for lesbian sisterhood is never going to change that fact.

And here's another one: We're animals. More than that, we're primates. We are not really programmed for logic, or for personal growth, and we are especially not programmed for sisterhood. We are programmed to perpetuate the gene pool. Our body tricks us emotionally through a bunch of chemicals it releases in the brain so we will mate early and often. And our brain also can trick us into being attracted to and impressed by alpha behaviors, because that's good for the gene pool. Now, sisters, we know that both of these things can ruin our lives, so we have to become smarter than our biology.

And there's something else that Sister Carolyn believes we may well have in our primate programming. We may well have primitive programming in our DNA to be nasty to other females. That's pretty common in the primate world. It's not personal; it's an evolution thing, a species thing. Now, of course, there are the bonobos. The female bonobos get around that by being sexual with other females... which gets all those falling-in-love chemicals going, so they have a whole system of female bonding. Now, I don't want to get too sentimental about this bonobo thing, because it's about younger females showing subservient behavior to older females... and because these observations have only been made in captivity... So we're not going to go there. But my point is this: We would be

36

fairly unusual in the primate world if we naturally bonded with other females.

So I think that the J-word is scary for two reasons. First, it threatens our ideology, which is the ideology of sisterhood, of equality, of bonding between women to overthrow the patriarchy. Deeply cherished dreams and visions, sisters. I don't know a single feminist activist who does not have a profound investment in that dream. And second, the J-word makes us look at root causes, and that might bring us smack up against biology, which is a tough opponent. Tough, but not impossible, sisters.

And we know that not naming something does not make it go away. It can make it more or less invisible. We know that. But being invisible is not the same as not existing. So when we are afraid to admit the presence of jealousy among us, we do not make it go away. We make it tough to perceive and tough to confront. And when something is tough to confront, the discomfort does not go away, but our strategies for dealing with it get kind of convoluted.

Let's say someone is standing on your foot, but you are afraid to say, "Get off my foot." So you might explain politely how you need to move your foot... and you might want to make the case that being able to move your foot could benefit them. You might want to talk about the kind of people who lean on other people. You might want to talk about your special conditions that make it especially dangerous to have weight on your foot. Or you might say nothing until you have so much anger, you punch the person standing on your foot... still not confronting the issue.

This is what I see happening in our communities because we can't own the J-word. We say things like "She intimidates people." Well... what does that mean? That she walks around with a club in her hand? Or that she perhaps uses language in a way that is seen as a marker of having a formal education? Or that she actually has some management experience that she is bringing to the table of a local collective? If it's the way she talks or the fact she actually has more experience, is she doing something aggressive... or is the woman who is feeling intimidated being triggered by reminders that we live in an unfair world?

Now, I know that most of y'all have done coalition work with other women, and maybe even with other lesbians. And I know you have heard folks complain about control freaks, and so on. And then there's a step above that, where folks will use language that is highly charged because it conjures up associations with violence against women. They will say that they were abused by someone who is on the committee, when what actually happened was that they were interrupted. They will say that someone has violated them, because they called for a vote instead of consensus. And this kind of thing can be very persuasive. Sometimes women don't realize that they are responding to the associations, instead of the actual situation. We all want to believe a woman who says she's been abused. We all want to show up as supportive, don't we?

And, let's face it, we are pretty adept at understanding oppression. We are very skilled at bringing our anti-colonialism, our anti-racism, our anti-ageism, etc. to the table... In fact, many of us are very adept at talking about oppression that comes from outside of ourselves. The problem is that we are not comfortable talking about the j-word, because that's an oppression that operates within our own skulls... possibly programmed in our DNA, and even more possibly hiding itself from our consciousness.

Who wants to own jealousy? It's like admitting to inferiority. "Oh, hell no. I'm not jealous of *her*." Well, sisters, sometimes I *am* jealous of her. Sometimes I am so jealous I can hardly contain myself. Sometimes I am so jealous, I can't stand it. Sometimes I can't WAIT to point out something—anything—she is doing wrong. I can get positively gleeful about it. "Gotcha!" Like maybe this sister wrote twenty books and cured cancer and built a rocket to the moon using parts of a blender, but if I can catch her doing anything wrong—maybe violating the blender?—then maybe that makes me smarter than her and I can get myself a little piece of her glory by trumping her accomplishments.

Well, of course I can't. Not really. I can get a momentary rush. But real life doesn't work that way. Maybe it feels like it's going to, but it doesn't. My calling out my sister with such obvious enthusiasm makes me look petty, that's what. Petty and jealous. And, sisters, here's a thing to keep in mind. My mean-spirited little "gotcha" might just possibly be a straw that breaks a camel's back. Women of accomplishment are human. Constant criticism can wear a person down, even if

39

they understand it's motivated by jealousy or fear. It's still negative and destructive. We may feel very proud of ourselves calling out some woman we envy. It might not occur to us that we could actually hurt her. But we can. It's actually a function of low-self-esteem on our part to think that our attacks will not hurt.

I want to talk a minute about Harry Houdini, the magician. I want to talk about how he died. On stage, he had this trick, where he would invite members of the audience to come up on stage and punch him in the gut as hard as they could. Of course, he would be braced for it, and he had amazingly powerful abdominal muscles. Houdini put a lot effort into working with his body. That's how he did some of his tricks. So here's an account of what killed him:

"On the afternoon of October 22, 1926, two McGill University students visited Houdini's dressing room. According to reports, Houdini was looking through his mail, when one of the students, J. Gordon Whitehead, asked Harry if he could indeed withstand any blow to the abdomen, as the magician had previously proclaimed. Harry responded that he could, if given time to brace himself, at which point Whitehead hit Houdini four times in the abdomen, under the impression that Houdini had indeed braced himself for the blows."

But here's the thing, sisters. Houdini had not braced himself. He was in his dressing room reading his damn mail. He was BACKSTAGE, not in the spotlight. He died a few days later of a ruptured appendix and peritonitis. His last words were, "I'm tired of fighting." Maybe he was tired of all the petty people who were always calling him out about his tricks, trying to find out how he did them, jealous of his success.

Why am I telling you this? Because lots of lesbian activists and artists are fighters... in the public arena. We are tough-minded, tough-talking... and when we go out and do our work, we are braced for the hatred, the misogyny, the homophobia, the non-stop attacks on our work and ourselves. Backstage, with our sisters, we are not braced for it. The same kinds of attacks coming at us backstage and when we aren't expecting them, can kill us. And often we are not expecting these attacks from our own sisters.

I remember attending a book reading event in San Francisco many years ago. One of the most brilliant lesbian theorists and activists in the world was presenting one of the world's first anthologies on lesbian culture. It was not an academic book, but a populist anthology. Sisters, all of those things were miracles in a homophobic patriarchy. And, of course, she had not been paid yet, and even when she got paid, it wasn't going to be much more than a stipend, because that's how it was in the world of lesbian publishing back then.

What I'm saying is that it was, like her lifework, a labor of love. Well, what happened? One of the contributors took to the stage to attack her... And this contributor was well prepared for the attack, but the author was not. The author was expecting a sister. Instead, this "sister" got up and repudiated her participation in the book, reaming it out for being classist and racist, and so on. It was an ambush. It was those four punches to Houdini's gut. The author, who lived with disability, was tired of fighting. Her response to this was to send a letter out to her colleagues announcing her permanent withdrawal from lesbian activism. And she meant it.

So, I know what you are thinking. You are thinking, "But were the accusations valid?" Yes and no. I challenge you to find any anthology with perfectly balanced inclusivity in terms of race, class, age, ability, regionality, and specific ethnicities. This was in the early years of lesbian publishing and it was not that easy to find authors willing to be publicly identified as lesbians. This was especially true if these authors were members of other marginalized communities. And, yes, there was a photograph that was insensitive. Could there have been better editorial vetting? Yes. And that is partly on the publisher.

But the attack was personal, public, and intended to devastate. Nobody benefited from it. And I am sure that, like the boys who attacked Houdini, the attacker had no idea the damage she caused. For her it was the rough-and-tumble of lesbian politics, and so on.... Only it wasn't. I was there and my perception was that the J-word was a huge factor. The author had a PhD. She had a book. Several books. That meant it was okay to attack with unfair advantage. Perhaps in the eyes of the attacker, that was a fair tactic, because the author seemingly had so much privilege.

Sisters... Those of us doing this work in the 1970's and 1980's know that our community was bristling with women ready to "correct" each other, and I put that word "correct" in quotes. We were ready to take down each other. And we did.

In little ways and in big ways. It could be scary to be a radical feminist.

One more story... Mary Daly. Her book *GynEcology* was groundbreaking... and guess what? It actually reflected the background and experience of the author... *quel surprise*. In reframing Western spiritual history, she referenced white European tradition. Yes, there was a lack of reference to African tradition, goddesses, and so on. Is that a significant omission? Yes, of course. AND did Mary Daly deserve to have her reputation destroyed over that? No.

And the way that came down was this: Audre Lorde wrote a letter confronting the white Euro-centrism of the book. Daly responded respectfully in a letter that, to me, appeared acceptably accountable. Lorde later published her letter and said that Daly ignored it, refused to respond, never wrote to her, never met with her, and so on. And Daly was marked as arrogant, racist, and "not getting it." After Lorde's death, her biographer discovered Daly's letter among Lorde's papers. It was a chilling moment. Had Lorde forgotten about it? Did she lie about it?

We can never know what her motive was. Her biographer struggled with her discovery. Maybe sometimes one's oppression can be so great and on so many fronts that it feels self-hating to dot the I's and cross the t's when we deal with others. But sisters, we need to do that, especially with our potential allies.

43

And why didn't Daly publicize the fact that she had indeed responded and responded conscientiously to Lorde's concerns? We can never know… except that, unless she had a copy of that letter, calling Lorde a liar would have been a dangerous move. What we do know is that Daly's reputation took a huge hit to the gut. From a sister. Much good work did not happen because of that. It was a loss to all lesbians, and to all women. And I invite you all to read the letter. It's published in *Warrior Poet*, the biography of Lorde by Alexis De Veaux.

I sometimes wonder if this whole queer movement that came in on the heels of radical feminism was in some ways a reaction to the j-word and our inability to own it and deal with it in our communities. I mean, think about it… The whole post-modern thing was all about how there is no truth, that all truth is relative or subjective… that, in fact, there is no such thing as "women," as "lesbians," even as "children," because these categories are all just social constructs. Maybe that ideology was just a huge relief to a generation of women who had watched their foremothers and big sisters rip each other to shreds, publicly and privately, and post-modernism meant they didn't have to live under that kind of scrutiny or with that kind of fear.

Sisters, this is something really important we need to grapple with. When we identify the patriarchy and when we reject it, we are doing something critical to our survival. And that process is a difficult one. We need to make sure we are not lying to ourselves about the degree to which that j-word might be motivating our critique. We need to understand that there is a difference between an analysis, which is about synapsing, and a judgment, which is about telling other people their business. And it's a fine line. Sometimes as thin as a hair. But it's there. It's always there, and it behooves us to locate that line and stay on our side of it. And, sisters, jealousy makes us overlook that line. Jealousy pushes us across it. We have to be honest with ourselves. Deeply, radically honest.

It's okay to be jealous. It's human. We're all jealous. Or at least capable of it. It's probably not going to go away. But we don't have to act on it. We don't have to pretend it's not there. We don't have to be afraid to notice it in other women. And the critique can have some validity to it—maybe even a lot of validity—and jealousy may still be a factor. When a confrontation or a critique is disrespectful in its dynamic, jealousy is probably the motivator. One of our best tools, our best warrior skills, can be to notice the method of delivery, the dynamic, BEFORE we engage with the content. If someone is using disrespectful language or dynamics... *that* should be the first thing on our response agenda. Just because the person confronting is focused on the error of our ways, that doesn't mean that we have to ignore blatant disrespect and scorched earth tactics.

Sisters, there is language for situations like these: "I need to ask you to lower your voice right now." "I am uncomfortable with the language you are using right now. Can you find another way to say this?" "I understand you are upset with my presentation, *and* this is my time on the stage. I will be happy to address your comments after I'm through." And so on.

45

At the Lesbian Tent Revival, we are in a voluntary and conscientious Sisterhood of the Sacred Synapse. We take our brains seriously, and we take responsibility for the connections we make with them... even when some of it is programmed in by biology or by the patriarchy. We *work* to make our brains serve us and serve the planet. And jealousy is a computer virus, my sisters. It's a computer virus of the brain. It's going to hack into our programs for sisterhood and activism, and it's going to do some serious damage. It's a worm. It weasels its way in under the guise of feminism. We have to debug our brains, run the anti-j-word software periodically and delete those viruses.

Jealousy is the Trojan horse of patriarchy. It's how we do the enemy's work among ourselves, and on ourselves. It is a hideous thing, sisters, to punish a woman for owning her own power. Let's take a page from twelve-step programs where they know the power of separating the self from the behavior. Let's not be afraid to stand up and say, " I am so-and-so, a good feminist and a Sister of the Sacred Synapse, and I am a jealous woman." Boom. "And" not "but." I am both of these things. And they are separate, and one does not operate under the guise of the other.

I am Sister Carolyn of the Sisterhood of the Sacred Synapse and I am a jealous woman. Today I can own that jealousy and I can use it to keep the focus on myself, instead of comparing myself with my sisters. I remember that all of us have more in some areas and all us have less in other areas. I use my jealousy to fuel my activism, but not to tear down my sisters. I work every day to communicate with respect, to identify that line between judgment and analysis, to take responsibility for my words and my actions... and *especially* when I am needing to confront. I own my jealousy and I override it with *conscientious* recognition of the achievements of my sisters, with verbal expressions of gratitude for their work, and with helping them achieve visibility... in a good way. I am Sister Carolyn and I am a jealous woman, and today that jealousy does not destroy my accountability, my trustworthiness, my alliances, and my own self-esteem. Blessed be.

Sermon on Mirrors and Firewalls

Sisters, in the Lesbian Tent Revival anthem, there is a line, "You can't stand still on a moving train." What does that mean? It means that even though you may not be moving on the train, you are still traveling in a direction, because the train is moving you. I have just come back from one of the three gated lesbian communities in the world. And it was an amazing thing to be in a village of five hundred lesbians. It was amazing and wonderful and all of the things you might expect it to be. And it was also saddening. And I will tell you why.

Because there were women there who could not use the word "lesbian." I mean, here they are, these lesbians in the middle of the Arizona desert who have come all the way out there just to live with other lesbians. I'm sure that nobody in that RV park was actually a local. These lesbians came there specifically to live with lesbians... to play pickleball, pool, poker, pingpong, bocsce ball... to potluck, to line dance, to hot- tub with other lesbians... and they can't say the word! And that's not all. Some of them don't want to attend anything having to do with lesbians. They don't feel like we are as talented as mainstream performers... or that there is any value in our stories.

Now, mind you... I'm not talking about all the women. There were many, many women there who were out and proud lesbian-feminists. But there were a lot of other women who had this other attitude.

And I want to talk about this. It's important. It's about mirrors and firewalls. Did you know that researchers on childhood trauma have found that the one of the most difficult forms of child abuse from which to recover is not what you might think. It's not physical violence and/or child sexual abuse. It's actually ignoring the child or invalidating them. That seems hard to believe until you think about it. A child is a child. They do not have fully formed brains yet. Their synapses are not making full connections and networks yet. They are still laying down the tracks. Children are very dependent on adults around them for helping them process information, helping them make sense of their perceptions, helping them figure out who they are.

When a child is ignored or invalidated, it's like they grow up with all the mirrors covered. They don't learn who they are, where they leave off and where another person starts... They don't know where their boundaries are. They don't learn the cause-and-effect of their own presence and power, because when they express a need they are ignored. It's like the question, "If a tree falls in the woods and no one hears it, is there sound?" No feedback, no mirroring, no closure, no validation. And if there is no sound, did the tree really fall?

So the child grows up with all kinds of gaps and weird connections. And having to figure all this stuff out as an adult can be really, really confusing. Especially because they might have learned all this wrong stuff... like that they don't have needs or feelings, that there is no point in articulating anything, that they are extensions of other folks, or that their job is serving others. That when they are serving others, that's is the only time they have presence, which is to say the only time they exist. Terrible confusion and existential pain.

And here's a really important point: Existential pain is one of the biggest triggers for suicidal ideation. Those folks jumping off the buildings in the Great Depression might not have been jumping because they lost their money. They might have jumped because they could not imagine their lives without money. Maybe they did not know who they were without their money. Maybe it was an existential identity crisis that killed them, not a financial one. Well... these ignored children grow up with that existential crisis big-time, because they never had a solid basis for their identity to begin with. They are very much at risk of having a fragile or incomplete sense of identity. And losing one's identity can be more painful and/or terrifying than losing one's life.

So what's my point? My point is this: Lesbians who can't bear to hear or use the word lesbian have something like this going on. They have been abused, but, unlike these ignored or invalidated children, their abuse is cultural and societal. The whole world ignored them and invalidated them. And us. And it still does. Even our own LGBT movement. Let's be clear about this. Our mirrors are always covered. Or, these days, replaced with images that don't look like us. The mainstream culture has a picture of what they wish a lesbian was, and they hold that up to us and say, "Look! It's a mirror! This is you!" And then some of us feel crazy, or confused, or enraged. Because we actually know what we look like, and we know this is not a frickin' mirror. And we know that this is an act of colonization. It's politically aggressive. It's got just enough truth for us to relate, so then we will swallow all the rest of it.

And I have said this before, but I want to say it again: Our enemies understand the power of ignoring and erasing us. They have always known it. This is not an accident or an oversight on their part and we are foolish if we want to frame it that way. Sisters, it is intentional. INTENTIONAL. And ignoring intentional acts of aggression against us is just stupid.

Anyway, I've said it before and I'm saying it again. And I'm going to read you a little something now... a little something from 1921, from the British Parliament... the House of Lords. What these Lords were discussing was lesbians. They had a law of gross indecency on the books to deal with gay male sexual behavior, but they didn't have any laws describing or dealing with lesbian behavior. And a case had come up regarding two women in Scotland who ran a boarding school... So suddenly they were wondering if they ought to have a law or something. They had already discussed incarcerating lesbians in lunatic asylums or even giving us the death penalty. But they decided against those measures, but not because they were too harsh. They decided that locking us up or killing lesbians might call too much attention to us, and then maybe women would start wondering what it was about women being intimate with each other that women would be willing to risk their lives for.

So listen up. This is what they decided... This is right out of the Parliamentary record. It supports my point that the lack of mirrors is an INTENTIONAL STRATEGY... Here is what they said:

> ...*to leave them entirely alone, not notice them, not advertise them. That is the method that has been adopted in England for many hundred years, and I believe that is the best method now, these cases are self-exterminating.*

They *know.* So, when you have an enemy and they have a specific, intentional strategy, you know what? You need to have a specific and intentional counter-strategy. *A specific, intentional counter-strategy.* We need one as a community, but we also need individual specific and intentional counter-strategies.

Now, I want to say that this business of abuse-via-ignoring is pernicious... that it is harmful in a subtle and gradual way. *Subtle and gradual.* That's one of the reasons why we have not been quick to devise counter-strategies. This abuse is like slow poison. And it's also difficult to spot, because our seeming allies also engage in this activity. I'm talking about gay men. They have universalized their issues and split off issues specific to lesbians as "women's issues" to be taken up by the National Organization for Women or by women's studies or something. They have ignored and erased us *as lesbians* in a movement that is supposed to be, at least in part, our own. And we have learned that it is disruptive to confront this with our gay brothers. We will find ourselves out in the cold, often ejected by other lesbians. We have learned to accept this invisibility as the price of coalition.

But when we ignore being ignored, we are actually contributing to our own oppression. It's exactly what they want us to do. Become, as the House of Lords so accurately put it, "self-eradicating."

So let's talk about filling our homes with mirrors that reflect our identity and our reality. How do we do that? Well, the first thing we have to do is inventory exactly how much space on our mental walls is being filled with these distorted or absent representations. How much TV, Hulu, Youtube, Netflix, DVD's do we watch? Because most of those erase us or lie about us. I know, sisters, I know... and this is considered recreational. I know. And maybe it is recreational... but it is not harmless. It's not harmless. Some folks refer to watching stuff like this as "brainless." But it's not. Connections are being made. We are turning over our precious synaptic wiring to idiot programmers who are interested in lowest common denominators... sex and violence. And, sisters, in order to follow along, we have to be using the same synaptic track as the screenwriter and the actors. We are laying mental rail even as we watch. Or, rather, it's being laid for us.

So let's do that inventory. How many hours a day do we spend consuming products that exclude, ignore, stereotype, invalidate us? A painful inventory. But "denial" is not a river in Egypt. And pretending that this is harmless and that's it's not affecting our thinking or the way we experience our lives or the choices we make is denial, pure and simple. Denial with a very high price tag. Like our happiness.

Let's go easy on ourselves, but let's go. Even if it's just moving forward a millimeter. Can we replace some of this time with something that empowers us, reflects our dreams, our visions for ourselves and for other women? And all that electronic media can work both ways. We can find amazing documentaries about women, and many of these are lesbians. Often these are free. Let's help ourselves and each other deprogram.

Sisters, the patriarchy incentivizes us powerfully to partake of its wares. For one thing, it can make us feel we belong, even as we are being excluded. We can talk about Downton Abbey at work. We can talk about the latest romantic comedy with our daughters. And of course, it's all very expensively produced and packaged. It's feels high quality… as opposed to some of our own home-grown products.

I remember hearing a lesbian tell me she likes to see plays with high production values. What that means is expensive sets and costumes in uptown venues. She wasn't saying that she hated lesbian theatre or that she would never support it. She was saying that, until such time as lesbian theatre can move into Equity theatres and afford five-and six-figure budgets, she would not support it. And what she was pretending, in the way she said it to me, was that it was just a question of lesbian theatre, and lesbian playwrights, becoming good enough to "make it" in the mainstream. Well, sisters, that's her fantasy that we are on a level playing field. The playing field is tipped so vertically against us that lesbians have to learn rock-climbing to play the game, whereas the patriarchal artists, just rappel themselves gracefully into those high-production value slots.

When the patriarchy makes its products so easy to access and so glitzy and glamourous, how can we incentivize ourselves to track down or make our own not-so-glitzy and glamorous cultural products? Well, that's actually a tough question.

This is what Sister Carolyn does: She studies up on lesbian herstory. She realizes how unique lesbians and our stories actually are. She understands that a lesbian got us Social Security and minimum wage and Medicare and the 40-hour workweek and workman's comp. She knows that a lesbian saved the planet from pesticides. She knows that a lesbian established the field of women's professional sports. She knows that a lesbian is the greatest poet in American literature. She knows these things and she knows that these lesbians achieved what they did BECAUSE of their lesbianism and not in spite of it or apart from it. She knows that if she cares about herself and about the planet, she needs to hold close the stories of these lesbians and the lessons from them, because they apply very directly to her own life and experience.

To incentivize ourselves to hunt down and to create the mirrors of our lesbian selves is work, sisters. It's the work of decolonization. It's the price of freedom. We help each other do it. We remind ourselves to do it.

And here's a little side road: Photos. Some folks have a place in their home where they hang all the photos of their family. A mantle or a hall wall. There is power in that. Every time they see it, it reminds them of where they came from, who they are, of who shares their heritage with them, who cares about them, who thinks like them.

Sisters, not all of us had families that were family, if you know what I mean. Some of us had families that did not have our back... alcoholism or homophobia or whatever. Some of us had families that did not support us, did not understand us, did not reflect our values, and so on.

Well, sisters, if that's your story, then here's a tip: Get that photo gallery going with a different family. Hunt up the pictures of the folks, living or dead, famous or not, who DO feel like family. Even if they don't know you, you can know them. And frame them, or attach quotations to them, and then put them all in some place where you are going to look at them every day. There is tremendous power in that. It's subtle, but persistent, and it works like water carving into a stone. Sister Carolyn did that thirty years ago, and eventually she became friends with many of the women whose photos she was looking at. It's like a miracle. But it starts with affirming, "Here is my family. Everyone is entitled the power and comfort of family, and here is mine." Try it. Mirrors, sisters, mirrors.

And the more the patriarchy attempts to erase, distort, or appropriate our images and representations... the more that tells us that they recognize how powerful we are. Do they know something about us that we don't? Sisters, if they are burning us as witches, just maybe we do have supernatural power... at least compared with them! If they fear our power so much, then let's figure out what it is and how to use it!

So... firewalls. Firewalls are a computer term. A firewall is a part of a computer system or network that is designed to block unauthorized access while permitting outward communication. The patriarchy has a lot of firewalls. It communicates to us. It tells us who we should be and what we should think. But when we try to see who or what is behind that, we run into firewalls. Sisters, there is a huge amount of our stolen history behind that firewall. Never forget that.

And because the patriarchy has firewalls, we have run into them unknowingly, we have internalized some of these. I am thinking of those lesbians who go to live in the middle of the desert in a village of lesbians, but they can't stand to hear the word. They have a firewall in their brain. They have a big part of their brain that is filled with homophobic propaganda. It sends messages out... it makes them flinch when they hear "the l-word." It makes them say "l-word" instead of "lesbian." But if they try to sit with themselves and look at why that is and where that fear came from, they are going to run into a firewall. They will find they can't access it. But it just keeps sending out the messages that are going to wreck their lives... or at the very least, keep them from realizing the power and joy of a fully-realized lesbian identity.

Dysfunctional families implant firewalls, too. "Thou shalt not feel, thou shalt not tell, thou shalt not trust." But when we go to figure out why we shouldn't feel, tell or trust... there's that damn firewall again. We are not allowed to see the inner workings behind these toxic little memos that are being sent down our synapses all the time. Because if we did, we would see, like Dorothy in the *Wizard of Oz*, the little man behind the curtain.

We can be incentivized not to feel, not to think radically, not to tell or to trust. But we can outsmart the man behind the curtain. We can counter-incentivize ourselves to do all those things. We can reward ourselves every time we do those things that our conditioning punishes us for. We can find new communities who will say, "Good for you" and "Thank you" when we name the perpetrator. We can treat ourselves, because that's not being selfish or wasteful. It's a great use of resources. We can put our picture up on the family wall of truth-tellers and proud lesbians. We can actually teach our brains to give us little endorphin rushes for doing the things that help us reclaim ourselves.

Lesbian community is essential to incentivizing our liberation behaviors. We have way too much of this rugged individualism in our culture. The patriarchy loves it when we are proud of our toxic individualism. The patriarchy hates interdependence. It wants utter dependence on itself AND toxic self-sufficiency. Sisters, it's good to need each other. And it's also tough to have made it a priority in one's life to be self-sufficient in all things. When we do that, we're going to find that we will usually be harboring a touch of contempt for those who need others and who ask for help. Self-sufficiency can hide a huge firewall of patriarchal propaganda machinery.

Too few mirrors and too many firewalls. Moving train of patriarchy. It's going to take action, sisters, to counter these. We absolutely must incentivize our liberation. We have to incentivize our liberation more than the patriarchy is incentivizing our denial. That's a tall order. Good thing we're dykes, right?

And I think about the epidemic of depression. Sisters, what if depression is a side effect of firewalls? What if something is generating toxic messages and feelings all the time, and we are blocked every time we try to figure out where these messages are coming from? We get tired, we get frustrated, we blame ourselves, we give up. Eventually we may become clinically depressed.

Well… firewalls are tough to dismantle. Maybe it's more productive to put our energy toward building our own communication centers and networks—ones that will send down radical, inspiring, invigorating, revolutionary, memos… LESBIAN and FEMINIST memos reminding us that it's the patriarchy that's stealing our joy and our courage. What if we start broadcasting and celebrating our achievements? What if we start taking our ideas and encouraging ourselves and each other to run with them?

If trying to get behind the default patriarchal firewalls is like running into a brick wall, then let's just out-broadcast the damn thing. Let's just let it keep broadcasting, because we're not listening anymore. It can keep its little secret identity. It can keep its nasty secrets. It can keep sending its vicious memos. Nobody's paying attention anymore. Because we are getting far more validation, far more rushes from ourselves and from our sisters for paying attention to our rich and joyous lesbian identity, history, culture and lives!

Blessed be!

Sermon for a New Year

Well, Sisters, this is that time of year when everybody's supposed to be starting fresh, with a clean slate... making a bunch of resolutions for the New Year. And I guess that's what the ministers are preaching about this week, so Sister Carolyn's been giving some thought to it, too. To New Year's Resolutions.

And it made me think about vision. Two kinds of vision, if you look up the word in the dictionary. There's seeing what's around you. That's the first one. And then there's seeing into a "fanciful future." That second definition seems a little cynical to me. "Fanciful future." Visions of the future are not necessarily fanciful. They can be damned serious things. And they can change the present. We all know that. See yourself a certain way down the line, and it gets a whole lot more likely that's who you're going to be. So anyway... two kinds of vision.

And those two kinds of vision are kind of like eyesight. Near-sighted... seeing right in front of you with a lot of clarity, but things in the distance are kind of fuzzy... and far-sighted where you can see things that are in the distance in sharp focus, but things up close are kind of blurred.

We are a near-sighted culture these days, sisters. Near-sighted. And because of that, we have put our future in jeopardy. We can see what's in front of our face. We can see the laundry that needs to be done this week, and the job we have to get to in an hour, and we can see the groceries that need buying... but it's a little fuzzier about how this planet is going to survive all the things we've done to it so we can do all these things that we're doing today the way we're doing them.

We are encouraged to be near-sighted. We are incentivized for it, in fact. And we are punished for being far-sighted. Far-sighted activists can get themselves locked up. They can be ridiculed, marginalized. But, worse than that, far-sighted folks disincentivize themselves. That is true. Get up in the morning and look outside at that fresh dew or fresh snow or new leaves... and think about global warming, and acid rain, and genetically modified seeds and electromagnetic radiation and that big continent of trash in the middle of the Pacific and all the species becoming extinct and the ozone layer... and it's enough to make your brain shut down altogether. Or send you back to video games or your grocery list or something like that.

Two D's, sisters. Two D's. We live our lives between the poles of the two D's: Despair for the long term and distraction for the short term. There has never been so much cause for despair for the future and there have never, never, never, ever been so many opportunities for distraction. Computers, sisters. Computers. And Netflix and Hulu and Cable and Digital TV, and laptops, and iPads, and iPhones and email and text messaging and Facebook and Twitter and Youtube. You can spend your whole day in fantasy worlds and disembodied conversations... and many of us find that our jobs require us to do that even if we don't want to.

We read the news, and there is some new horror right there next to a fascinating article about the world's largest mushroom. We're going to go for the mushroom, because the horror's just going to overwhelm us, and we're kind of curious about that big mushroom. Curious in a way that we aren't curious about atrocity. So which article are we going to click on? So our human nature is conspiring to dumb us down, too.

Despair and distraction. Far-sight and near-sight. And if you had to choose one, wouldn't you be an idiot to choose despair? But wouldn't you also be another kind of idiot to choose distraction? For this new year, I'm going to repeat a quotation by lesbian poet Mary Oliver:

> *"Tell me, what is it you plan to do*
> *with your one wild and precious life?"*

And the answer might be: "Force myself hourly to face the realities of planetary destruction brought on by human greed and stupidity." Or it might be: "Allow myself a lifetime of distraction with pleasant and mildly satisfying artificially manufactured and manipulated challenges."

Neither one of those really speaks to a "wild and precious life," do they? What are we going to do, with this new year in front of us… this wild and precious, yet-to-unfold new year?

Well, sisters, I am thinking about Harriet Beecher Stowe. And someone once asked her a question that had to do with those two poles: despair and distraction. It was during the time when half of the country was practicing legal enslavement of descendents of people forcibly abducted from Africa... It was a huge evil, entrenched in practice and in law and in the economy. Lots of people were trying to figure out ways to stop it without financial ruin and bloodbaths. Lots of folks got overwhelmed thinking about it. So they would ask Harriet about it, because she was an abolitionist. They wanted to know what one person could do... And often they were all ready to argue with whatever she would answer, to prove that it wasn't going to do any good anyway. Because that's an easy argument to make in the face of a massive institutionalized social or environmental evil.

But Harriet was too smart for those arguers. She answered with this:

"But what can any individual do? Of that, every individual can judge. There is one thing that every individual can do—they can see to it that they *feel right*.

And she would emphasize those last two words: *feel right*. She would put them in italics.

That's a very synaptically savvy response. "See to it that you feel right." Very canny. Because what she's really saying is "see to it that you stay present." See to it that you don't use the overwhelming sense of evil of enslavement as an excuse to practice distractions. See to it that you don't get so frozen over the sense of your own impotence that you just turn off your brain to the injustice. You stay present. You stay aware. You see to it that you feel right. You make sure you don't turn your eyes away, you don't turn your heart off, you don't go up in your head and play in some fantasy world. You stay present, you stay aware, you stay in your damn body, you stay in touch with your emotions, and you hang with the discomfort. The WILD discomfort of the facts of this enslavement. Because she knew that a commitment to feeling right about a situation was going to bring change, in the individual and in the country.

What can we do about the drones being deployed in our undeclared wars? We can see to it that we feel right, that we understand the number of casualties and that we make the effort to know who those casualties are.

And part of that feeling right is not to allow it to overwhelm us. We're not being asked to fix it... just to *feel right.* Which is to say: Stay present.

Sisters, that is a radical act. That is THE radical act. That is what the forces of this culture are arrayed against at this time. Everything is conspiring to see that we are not present. That we are dissociated and disembodied, distracted, absent, daydreaming... or worse yet, dreaming a Hollywood dream.

You know, sisters, we have morphed into a visual culture. That's right. We used to be a spoken-word culture. But now we are in a culture of moving image. Moving image makes it easier to impose connections onto our brains without our conscious permission. Thousands, millions of connections and in the blink of an eye. Oral arguments required more participation, more conscious permission. We would follow the synaptic tracks of an oral argument as they were getting laid down. Now we just open our eyes and we find that those synaptic tracks are already laid down... without our permission or our participation. We are losing our freedom of thought, our autonomy. The Constitution guarantees us "freedom of association"... and sisters, the association between neurons is the foundation of that freedom. And we are losing it a mile a minute. We have become highly vulnerable to manipulation. We often mistake meaningless motion for authentic movement. We jiggle instead of journey. Sisters, we have to stop that. We have to get back on the path. We have to chart those journeys again. We have to get going.

How do we do that? We take Harriet's advice, her challenge, her admonition: We see to it that we feel right. And how do we keep the state of the world from overwhelming us? By sticking strictly to her job description: feeling right. We don't have to fix the world. We don't have to even figure out how someone else should fix it. That's a job beyond our pay grade in this life. We don't have to rescue anyone or anything. That's where the overwhelm, the burden of guilt and responsibility takes over and pretty soon we're back to video games.

We just have to feel right. And then we have to trust the immense synaptic wisdom of our bodies, our whole bodies— brain included—to mobilize in whatever way is organic, correct, in line with our purpose and appropriate to our resources to incorporate and respond to that right-feeling. We just send the memo of right-feeling down the line, that ancient line of our DNA, not our young, programmed, ego-driven, incredibly recent thinking. Send it down the ancient DNA wisdom pipeline to our deep, inner truth. Talking about trust here. We make sure we feel right, and then we trust what our spiritual self is going to do with that information. The hard job belongs to inner wisdom. Our job is relatively easy: just to stay present.

Do you hear what I'm saying? I'm saying that there is a resolution this year that will save our lives and may save the planet. It's simple, it's do-able, and it is the single most dangerous and radical thing that any one of us can do. To stay present. To see to it that we feel right. And to allow the wisdom of the body to keep us from becoming overwhelmed with despair or burned out with ego-driven activism so that we come lured by the shallow relief of distraction

Sisters, stay present. Stay fully synapsing. Stay open, stay innocent, stay wise, stay canny. Listen and learn and relearn and keep learning. Talk and keep talking. Less Facebook, more face time. Less texting, more contexting. If we stay present, we will find whole universes opening up to us, all kinds of missions that are not going to overwhelm, that will meet us exactly where we are. We will find our purpose. We will find ourselves equipped for these journeys, because we will be connected with sources of supply that are invisible to us in our despairing or distracted modes. It's a simple formula: Stay present, see to it that we feel right. And trust the web of synaptic and biophilic connection to place and equip us for the work.

Not always comfortable. But that's okay. We can all handle some discomfort when it's compensated by that power of connection to deep truth and inner wisdom.

So, that's it, sisters. That's it for the New Year. May it be a meaningful year, chocked and loaded full of meaning and purpose. And how can you make sure it is that kind of year? By taking Harriet's advice. See to it that you feel right. Sisters, y'all stay present!

Blessed be!

Sermon on Logotherapy

Sisters, this is a sermon that I wrote as a kind of response to the publication of the DSM-5. Now, what is the DSM-5, and why is the Lesbian Tent Revival bothering to respond to it? Well, sisters… it is the *The Diagnostic and Statistical Manual of Mental Disorders.* That's the "DSM." The "5" refers to the fact that it is the Fifth Edition. They keep needing to update it. But what is it? Well, here's what Wikipedia has to say about it: "In the United States, the DSM serves as the principal authority for psychiatric diagnoses."

And in case folks don't quite get what that means, Wikipedia goes on to further elucidate: "Treatment recommendations, as well as payment by health care providers, are often determined by DSM classifications, so the appearance of a new version has significant practical importance."

Yeah. It means that this DSM-5 thing has the naming power… and sisters, you know that at the Lesbian Tent Revival we spend a lot of time talking about the power that comes from being able to name things. A lot of time. Right there in the Bible… Adam getting that power to name. Downhill from there. So the DSM-5 has the power to name mental disorders. And we have talked about this before. We have a whole sermon about "Delusional Dominance Disorder, which is absolutely a mental disorder. "Too big for your britches." But of course, it's not in the DSM, because that would kind of pull the covers on all kinds of politicians and corporate muck-a-mucks and domestic abusers who think they are entitled to control other people and other forms of life and all kinds of things. "DDD." "Delusional Dominance Disorder." And in that sermon we consider the implications of having DDD officially named a mental disorder. The implications, especially, for women, for cultural minorities, for colonized folks.

There's a lot of power in naming things. And especially in getting to name what is and what isn't mental illness. And then, not just naming it, but getting to decide how to treat it. Now, Wikipedia is careful to say that the DSM just makes "treatment recommendations," but then in the very same sentence it says, "as well as payment by health care providers." Yeah. It may just "recommend" a treatment, but if that recommendation is the only thing that insurance will cover, it's pretty much like a mandate for most of us. As I said, a lot of power.

So this sermon was written to respond to the release of this brand new edition of the DSM. They have to keep releasing new versions, because the culture is changing all the time, and as the culture changes, so does what we consider mental illness. What was considered crazy last year may be considered perfectly sane this year. And vice versa. The DSM is always controversial, and sisters, it is highly political. There was a time when women falling in love with women was considered mental illness instead of the optimal synapsing that it so clearly represents under patriarchy.

The DSM. The *"Diabolically Strategic Manual."* That's another name for it. A Lesbian Tent Revival name.

So, this publication of the DSM-5 sent me off looking for another school of psychotherapy, because no point in talking trash about something if you haven't got a better idea about how to get the job done. So I went looking and I found another school of psychotherapy, and that school is going to be the subject of this sermon. The name of that school is "logotherapy."

Logotherapy was developed by a man named Victor Frankl. He was a psychologist and a neurologist and a Holocaust survivor... and he thought a lot about mental health and he thought a lot about suicide. Part of that is because he survived Dachau, but also before the war, he had worked in a psych hospital in Vienna in something called the Selbstmörderpavillon, or the "self-murder pavilion"... the suicide unit. He treated over thirty thousand women who had a penchant for "selbstmörder." So from an objective clinical point of view and a subjective "been-there-done-that" point of view Victor Frankl had a tremendous understanding of human suffering. And he founded a school of psychotherapy after the war and after he got out of Dachau, and he named this school "logotherapy."

Now, I don't hear people talking about logotherapy these days. It's been around for eighty years, but hardly anybody knows about it. These days, people talk a lot about Big Pharma, and they talk about the DSM, and they sure talk a lot about insurance... but I don't hear them talking about logotherapy. And you know, sisters, any time the patriarchy isn't talking about something, you best go hunt it up and figure out why, because it might just be the very thing you need in order to be whole.

So why is it that nobody is talking about logotherapy? Why is it that nobody seems to know anything about a school of therapy founded by a man who specialized in suicidal ideation, and then actually went to hell and survived and came back sane. Suicide is epidemic these days. So why don't we know this school of therapy? Well, I'll tell you. It's because it's a therapy based on the belief that the primary, the most overwhelming motivating and driving force in humans is to find a meaning in one's life. Yeah. How about that? *Living a meaningless life as a cause of mental illness.*

And what if that meaninglessness in one's life is behind a whole lot of that depression and anxiety and mood-swinging and insomnia and obsessions and compulsions and addictions that make up that DSM. What if underneath and behind all of that is the fact that people are having trouble finding any meaning in their lives?

And I wonder what would happen if they put "living a meaningless life" in the DSM-V as a form of mental illness? I bet you more than half of the people in America could file for disability! Just picture that official diagnosis: "Patient appears to be engaged in meaningless work." Or "Patient indulges in mindless consumption." But meaningless life, meaningless work... those are things that kind of fuel the whole economy. That is not something anybody wants to look too hard at, unless it's the Lesbian Tent Revival.

And I think we should look at that. And I think we should look at logotherapy. We've got schools of psychotherapy that are based on drives for power, and we've got schools of psychotherapy based on drives for pleasure. But "meaning"… sisters, what about "meaning" as a primary drive?

If you have a drive for power, where's that going to leave you when you find yourself impaired? Or when you find yourself on hard times where you don't have those resources that give you so much control? And if you have a drive for pleasure, where's that going to leave you when you get bored or numb to the things you used to enjoy? But, see meaning… well, if you are on a search for meaning, that's something that can really tide you over. That's something that's really forward thinking. It's not retrospective or introspective or tail-chasing or naval-gazing as some of the therapy is today. And Victor Frankl was aware of this difference. In fact, he used to make a joke about it… Of course, this was decades ago and some things have changed, but you can still get the gist. He'd say, "Well, traditional therapy is where you lie on a couch and say disagreeable things, and logotherapy is where you sit in a chair and hear disagreeable things."

So, I would maybe update that a little bit… get rid of the couch and the chair and say that traditional therapy is based more on personal family secrets, and that maybe logotherapy is based more on the cultural, or societal, or institutional family secrets, because logotherapy identifies two kinds of neurosis. One is psychogenic… that is, it takes place in your own brain. The other is noogenic, which means it comes from existential causes, like being required to do something in the workplace that's unethical. That situation is going to cause a neurosis... unless and until your brain has been completely colonized or you are handy at dissociation.

Logotherapy will call that a "noogenic neurosis"... something coming from existential frustration. And "existential frustration" is just a fancy phrase for a situation impossible to live with and remain sane. Anyway logotherapy doesn't pretend that this is something you are going to be able to fix by talking about your alcoholic family... although that might be useful in understanding how you are responding to the job situation. But the bottom line is that your mental distress is coming from the fact you have a job that's asking you to take care of yourself by violating yourself. It's an inherently crazy-making situation.

Logotherapy means you might be sitting in the chair having to hear that you might just need to leave that job if you want to have good mental health.

Victor Frankl also noticed something very important. He noticed that tension can be a good thing... like that tension between who you are today and who you might become. He said the tension between those two things is a good thing. It's a challenge. Challenge is a good thing. He disagreed with the idea that being in a perfectly balanced state, or being in a tensionless state or having no stress at all was good for people. Dr. Frankl discovered that this lack of tension is not good for mental health.

Sisters, we have become a comfort-driven culture. And Sister Carolyn feels that keenly in her alternate identity as a playwright. Folks don't want art that challenges us anymore. We want to be comforted, or numbed. We want formulas, which is what you feed to infants. We want formulas in our art. Familiar, predictable, reassuring, comfortable. Comfort can be commodified. And that means it can be monetized… and so there you are. If something stresses you out, give it up. Don't wrestle with it, don't hold onto it until new possibilities or new abilities emerge. And you know that Sister Carolyn believes that when the world says, "Pick A or B," it usually means that there is a "C: None of the Above" that is hidden from view, and if you can just stand the tension, the stress of holding out, you can bring it into being. And often that "C," is often packed with meaning… both personal and cultural. And some of that meaning comes from the fight you had to put up to arrive at it.

Let's ask ourselves if we are responding to the call for discovering personal meaning. You know Rachel Carson, that wonderful lesbian marine biologist…? Well, she adopted her niece's five-year-old son when the niece died and nobody else stepped up to take the boy. She didn't have a maternal bone in her body, and she was at the height of her creative powers… getting ready to write some *magnum opus* about the history of all life on the planet… and suddenly here's this traumatized little boy knocking on her office door every few minutes. And, sisters, she wrote about it.

She wrote about it to her girlfriend who was, by then, a grandmother. She wrote about how it was driving her crazy, how she didn't know what to do... She wrote about her suffering. Sisters, she was stressed by that child. There was tension in her body, tension in her home, tension in her brain between her wild creativity and her grinding domestic duties.

But she stayed with it, because it was the right thing, the responsible thing, the ethical thing. And it changed her. Sisters, she got a vision of the connection between all living beings, and the responsibilities we have toward those other beings. You don't just wipe out all the mosquitoes because they bother you... because they are connected to so many other forms of life, and whatever kills them will kill the birds and then you've got your "silent spring." And *Silent Spring* was the book she ended up writing, instead of the one about the history of all life. It's not a huge book, but it's concentrated. It's the book that talks about the dangers of pesticides to the entire planet. It's the book that started the modern environmental movement. Some folks say it's the book that saved the planet.

You don't kill off all the mosquitoes with chemical aerial spraying and you don't dump your niece's child into foster care, because you are a famous writer. You wrestle with your priorities. You look for meaning in your suffering. And trust me, Rachel Carson was well aware that most men in her situation would have not taken on that child, and furthermore nobody would have expected them to. They would not have given it a second thought. But she did. And she suffered. And she wrote about that suffering, and she wrestled with it... and she held onto the child and she held onto her dream about writing a book that would change the way people saw the world... and what she got was one of the most influential books ever written.

And Victor Frankl would have understood that. Her stress, her tension enhanced and widened her search for meaning far beyond her original plans.

Now, I'm not saying go out there and stress yourself. But what I am saying is "look at it." Just look at the source of tension. Does it have anything to do with the things you find meaningful? Responsibility was important to Rachel Carson, and she felt she had a responsibility to use her gifts as a writer to communicate about nature, which she had a passion for. So being a parent was putting her in conflict with her meaningful work and sense of purpose. But as she wrestled with it, she saw that what she loved about nature was being extended to her taking responsibility toward this little boy. And then she saw that her guardianship also extended back to all of humankind's relationship to the natural world. Her either/or tension caused her perspective to grow so huge it took all of these things in together. The meaning of her life continues to change the world because she was willing to wrestle with her tension, to suffer, and to forge meaning in that suffering.

Frankl, talking about this tension thing, used the example of architects or engineers trying to shore up a kind of decrepit arch... how by loading more weight onto the arch, it can strengthen it. Instead of taking the rocks off it, because of the way an arch is built, you can put more on top to tighten it up and strengthen it.

People can spend their whole lives drifting around in this culture, feeling existential stress, not understanding exactly where it's coming from or what to do with it... feeling fragile and vulnerable and decrepit maybe... But what if we are really structured to seek meaning. Structured like that arch. Load on that search for meaning, and now the tension and the stress strengthen us.

Frankl says that this drive to find meaning is greater than the drive to find power or to find pleasure, and that when people can't find meaning in their lives, that's when they go hunting up the power—and when I say "power," I'm talking about how the culture defines it... power as control and domination... because of course real power is something else entirely. But that's another sermon.

So... living a life driven by a search for domination or distraction... according to logotherapy, those are symptoms of not being able to find real meaning in life. They are actually symptoms of poor mental health!

Dr. Frankl does not tell us what the meaning of life should be for us. He says that nobody can tell anybody that. It's the most personal thing in the world. And he says it changes. Here's an example he gives of that... He uses an example of a student talking to a master of chess. And this student asks, "Master, what is the best chess move in the world?" There's no answer to that, because it depends on the game. You have to look at the whole board, which is changing all the time. What might have been a good move two moves ago, might be a foolish move right now. And that's how it is finding meaning in one's life.

And here's something else that's very interesting about logotherapy. Two things, actually. One of them was what Dr. Frankl called "hyper-reflection." What is "hyper-reflection?" Well, it's thinking about something too much... Wanting something so badly, you can't possibly get it. So how does logotherapy treat this? Well, with something they call "de-reflecting." What is "de-reflecting?" Getting a bigger goal. Let's take a lesbian example here. We're all women in patriarchy. We've all had our sexuality affected by this, by the rape culture that propagates patriarchy. Most of us have or have had anxiety about how we are in bed.

Well, let's say there's a lesbian who hyper-reflects on this issue. She compares herself to what she sees in films, yes, even lesbian films. She compares her looks to that of other lesbians. She worries about her technique. She maybe has to fight her post-traumatic responses in bed, from something hideous that happened in her past. She doesn't want to be a downer for her partner, but, on the other hand, she can't help it. And her brain just goes around and around this squirrel cage. "I want to, but I can't. I can't but I want to." And the more she thinks about it, the more self-conscious and insecure she gets and on and on and on... until she scares everybody away before they even have time to ask her about her astrological sign.

So, logotherapy might tell her to de-reflect... to get a bigger goal. Like intimacy. And of course, intimacy is about authenticity and respect... starting with self-respect. The tools are not going to be vibrators. They're going to be self-awareness and good communication. Now, if she starts putting her energy there instead of on her appearance and what she thinks good sex should look like, she's going to find she can actually get off the hamster wheel. She is not going to be experiencing serial failures that reinforce the hyper-reflection. She may find she's still going through potential partners a-mile-a-minute, but it will be in a progressive, weeding-out kind of way that is productive in terms of her growth. It won't be failure.

So there's this other thing that Dr. Frankl named: "anticipatory anxiety," where you dread something so badly you bring it right into your experience. Now, in logotherapy, there is a technique called "paradoxical intention," and that is where you go ahead and intentionally call in whatever it is that scares you so much. With paradoxical intention, you face that fear. You go right out and beard that lion in the den. And this can resolve the anticipatory anxiety.

Does this mean you go fill your bed up with spiders? No. But it might mean that you go camping... which maybe you haven't done because you're so afraid of running into spiders. Maybe have some kind of plan for what happens if you do run into one, but go on out there and see if the spiders are really going to be the huge issue you might be dreading... and also see if there might be other rewards and qualities in that experience that might make the spider encounter not the big deal-breaker that you have been feeling it might be.

Dr. Frankl said that, using these techniques, you don't necessarily have to go through all that introspection and that inventory of every single bad experience you ever had. He said that sometimes these logotherapy techniques could just move you past something. And you have to remember, Dr. Frankl survived Dachau. He could have filled up a zillion journals about his traumatic experiences. How many hours of talk therapy would it take to "work through" all those memories? How many EMDR sessions per atrocity would it take?

But instead, he wrote *Man's Search for Meaning*. That was the book that gave meaning to his suffering, purpose to his life after Dachau. That was the book that brought healing. So, I think he knew what he was talking about. It's not a magic wand that logotherapy waves over all our trauma histories. It's a "cut to the chase" therapy that goes to the heart of what we need to do to reclaim and integrate these terrible experiences that are ours, whether we like it or not. It is a therapy that helps us empower ourselves by finding meaning in our suffering.

So the more I looked into logotherapy, the more I thought, "This is something that everybody ought to consider." And I had some trouble figuring out why nobody ever heard of it. And then I got to this part of it. So listen up.

Dr. Frankl said that life offers us meaning. "Offers." Doesn't give it to us. "Offers." Like someone standing there holding something in an outstretched hand, but we have to walk up and take it. We have to be active. He says life offers everyone purpose and meaning. It's an equal opportunity offer. Doesn't matter how hard your life is, or how easy, or how much privilege you have, or how much oppression you suffer. Life offers everybody purpose and meaning.

Which is a good thing, because Dr. Frankl tells us that the Number One drive is the drive to achieve meaning. And, in the same breath, Dr. Frankl tells us that life does not owe us a sense of fulfillment or happiness. It's really important to keep those two things linked together: "Life offers everyone purpose and meaning, and it does not owe anyone a sense of fulfillment or happiness." Wow.

I find that mind-boggling. I am not entitled to happiness or fulfillment. I am mind-boggled, because it seems to me that everything in this culture is telling all of us all the time that that is the way to mental health. And here is this psychologist, who, in my opinion has a ton of mental health credibility, and he is telling me, "Nope. You are not entitled to that." Sisters, after I read that, and had a little time to unboggle my mind, I actually felt a sense of relief.

It is this damn pursuit of happiness that is relentless and remorseless—relentless and remorseless, sisters. It makes you feel like you're missing something all the time... what is that expression... "FOMO?" "Fear of missing out." Makes you feel like other people are having this thing that you should be getting. And it does something else. It makes you get inattentive about who's paying for your happiness.... consuming shit that is destroying the environment. The "live for today" thing... Sisters, it makes us restless and irritable.

Like addicts. Because feeling you have a right to happiness fosters addiction.

And sisters, it's built into our government. The right to the pursuit of happiness. Right there in the Declaration of Independence. "Life, liberty and the pursuit of happiness." What if it was "life, liberty, and the pursuit of purpose and meaning?" Maybe we built the whole foundation of this country on the wrong thing. Sounds like a lovely idea, but it could be somebody wanting to buy women's bodies, or amass a huge fortune... just all kinds of crap. And, remember, that Declaration of Independence was written when slavery was legal and women were disenfranchised. People of color and white women were financing this "pursuit of happiness" for others. Nobody can finance a search for meaning for somebody else. That's a beautiful thing.

Anyway, you can see why corporate capitalism loves to take for granted that it's a good thing to feel entitled to anything that makes us happy... whatever the hell that would be, because the corporate capitalists can probably find a way to monetize that and sell it to us, at our own expense of course. And it also loves the idea of entitlement to fulfillment. We are entitled to be filled full. We are entitled to engorge ourselves. Oh, don't even get me started. But this is one of those little clues about why you never hear about logotherapy. Why, in spite of all our best efforts, mental health continues to get worse and worse and worse in our culture the more we are pursuing our happiness and fulfillment.

So, I just gotta say, I love what Dr. Frankl said: Life is offering all of us purpose and meaning, and it does not owe us happiness or fulfillment. Sounds kind of like a recipe for growing up, doesn't it?

Mary Daly had a lot to say about fulfillment. She saw fulfillment as an undesirable state for a feminist to be in... like maybe the way you feel after Thanksgiving dinner, where you just want to lie down and pass out.

So anyway... pursuit of happiness... not so much. And Dr. Frankl also had some very interesting things to say about freedom. He said that freedom was only "part of the story and half of the truth." He said that freedom was in danger of degenerating into mere arbitrariness. And that, sisters, defines our present moment politically. Arbitrariness. If the bottom line is money, and consumer fulfillment is the goal towards it... sisters, we are on a journey with no moral compass. Where we are going to end up is arbitrary. Wherever the winds of profit may dictate.

So let me go back and give you the rest of Dr. Frankl's sentence: "Freedom is in danger of degenerating into mere arbitrariness unless it is lived in terms of responsibleness." That is so important I am going to say it again: "Freedom is in danger of degenerating into mere arbitrariness unless it is lived in terms of responsibleness."

And I like that says "responsibleness," because "responsibility" just feels like some kind of burden... "Oh, now I'm responsible for this... I'm responsible for that." But

84

Dr. Frankl is saying that it is "responsibleness," not "responsibility."

And listen to this... I love this. Dr. Frankl recommended that the Statue of Liberty on the East Coast be supplemented by a Statue of Responsibleness on the West Coast. And that is a great idea, because when you couple up Lady Liberty in some kind of arranged marriage with pursuit of happiness, it just becomes license for greed and selfishness. And actually, you can look this up. There are folks who took Dr. Frankl seriously, and they have designed this statue. They call it the "Statue of Responsibility" instead of "Statue of Responsibleness"... maybe they weren't quite paying attention, but they have an interesting design. It's a statue that looks like two hands being clasped, like one hand pulling the other hand up out of the water. Kind of interesting. Don't know if they will ever raise the funds to build it, but we can hold it in our minds. We can know that freedom must always be coupled with that other half of the truth, which is responsibleness.

So, anyway... thinking about that DSM, that *Diabolic Strategic Manual* that can potentially have the power to tell us what's crazy and what isn't... I'm just going to suggest that if you haven't tried or looked into logotherapy, that maybe you should think about that. I think that logotherapy is really onto something here... that the key to mental health is focusing more on that search for meaning and not spending so much time focused on those lesser goals. What if the key to mental health is the challenge—yes, tension—and excitement of each person in their life having that ability, no matter who they are or what their circumstances, to find and experience meaning in their life?

Finally, Dr. Frankl talked about aging in a different way. He said that there were people who looked at aging like it was some kind of calendar that you tear off a page every day, and it just keeps having fewer and fewer pages. He suggests that we might, instead, see each of our days filled with meaning, so that as we get older, we just keep piling up this huge mound of meaning behind us, like a growing foundation for our life. This might just do away with that great fear of dying that informs our culture. We can look at our lives differently. We don't have to succumb to Dwindling Calendar Syndrome. We can see this richness of meaningful days filled with purpose as something that enlarges our living and moves us forward.

Dr. Frankl said something that I thought was interesting. He said, "If you know 'why,' you can put up with almost any kind of 'how.'" He was talking about having found meaning in life, in having a sense of why one was here... what one's purpose is. He is saying, once you have that sense of purpose, that understanding of "why," then whatever you have to do, no matter how painful, how difficult, how unfair... You can put up with it. Sisters, that is some powerful synapsing there. Might want to take that in, take that all the way in.

Blessed be!

Sermon on Toxic Self-Sufficiency

Today I'm going to be talking about one of the occupational hazards of being a lesbian. There are a lot of them, but this one is really a stealth occupational hazard, because it masquerades as something really wonderful, something to be proud of, something you can't have too much of. But you actually can, and so we're going to talk about it.

Funny how, sometimes in life, the cure can end up being worse than the condition it's supposed to fix. So… what am I talking about? Sisters, I'm talking about self-sufficiency. I know… I know. That's supposed to be a good thing. And for lesbians, that's historically been an especially good thing and even a necessity, because it meant we weren't going to have to depend on anybody, because when you depend on folks you find out that you have to please them, or do things the way they think you should… all that stuff. And that didn't usually include making love to other women. Many of us found out that, if we were going to live the lesbian lives we wanted, we would need to be pretty self-sufficient. And also that's been historically one of the great things about our lesbian partnerships. They tended to be more egalitarian than heterosexual partnerships, because nobody took for granted that one partner should be the breadwinner, and society wasn't set up to pay one partner automatically 30% more than the other for the same work. When two self-sufficient women came together to make a household, it could be a beautiful thing.

So why is Sister Carolyn preaching the evils of self-sufficiency? Well, because too much of a good thing is too much of a good thing. Too much self-sufficiency becomes toxic. It's like pouring Miracle-Gro fertilizer on a control freak. But it's also a situation where we can start to believe our own propaganda... not just personally, but also as an entire society or nation. And that can threaten the life of the planet.

So, today we're going to look at this self-sufficiency thing and look hard.

There was a great geo-scientist named Lynn Margulis. She died a few years ago and she is one of the great saints of the Lesbian Tent Revival. Saint Lynn Margulis. Why? Because she wrote a book that is even more important than Charles Darwin's book, *The Origin of the Species*. And there are a number of reasons why her book will never achieve the level of fame of *The Origin of the Species*... but that's not what I want to talk about, and besides, most of you can figure that out for yourselves. ANYWAY... her great book that no one will hear about is titled *The Symbiotic Planet: Evolution by Merger,* and what is great about this book is her theory of evolution, which she calls the "Gaia Concept."

Now, a theory of evolution is a theory that explains how things got to be the way they are. And a theory of evolution is packed with values... kind of like a form of religion. A theory of evolution presents a working model for the universe. That's why people can get so heated up over theories of evolution.

Like the creationists who insist that a big patriarch in the sky made the whole world in seven calendar days.

ANYWAY… the most commonly known and taught theory of evolution is the one by Charles Darwin. In 1859, Charles Darwin published *The Origin of the Species*, the book that made a monkey out of creation theory. Darwin's theory of evolution was about survival of the fittest: Random genetic mutations would lead to "natural selection," whereby the more rugged or adaptive species would multiply and be fruitful, while the less rugged, less adaptive species would die out. In other words, according to Darwin, competition was good for us.

This notion led to something called "Social Darwinism," a convenient rationale for the rampant and predatory capitalism that characterized the Industrial Revolution and which continues, under various guises, to manifest itself today. It's Social Darwinism to outsource our manufacturing to countries that have lower wages and fewer laws protecting the workers and the environment. It's Social Darwinism to pay lobbyists to get Congress to get rid of environmental regulations that cost money and slow corporations down. Competition, sisters. Competition as a natural order of the universe. Get tough or die out. Get ruthless or go out of business.

But, Margulis looked at the numbers, and they just didn't add up. In her book, she makes the point that genetic mutations, although common and easy to induce, rarely lead to changes that are beneficial to the organism. In other words, one's chances for becoming the lucky host of an advantageous change in DNA structure are considerably worse than those for winning the lottery—and the chances are even slimmer of becoming the founder of a new species, based on such a rare mutation.

So how *did* we evolve from pond scum, if it wasn't by Darwinian competition and natural selection?

Margulis argues that evolutionary advances are achieved, not by good genes and natural selection, but by a species' *success in achieving symbiotic mergers with other species.* And symbiosis means good for both parties... a dynamic that makes each partner stronger than they would be on their own. Wow. Couldn't be more opposite from rugged individualism and competition. *Success in achieving symbiotic mergers with other species.*

As I said, Lynn called her theory the Gaia Concept, and in scientific terms she defined it as a "serial endosymbiosis theory of evolution."

Okay. That's a mouthful. What does that mean in lay terms? Well, actually it means something pretty well understood by many lesbians. The Gaia Concept means that we evolve not by rugged individualism, but by relationships... and not just between plants and animals, but also between atmospheric gases, surface rocks, and water—all of which she maintains are regulated by the growth, death, integration and other activities of living organisms. In other words, it's about the entire ecosystem of the Earth's surface as a series of interacting ecosystems, which is definitely not your grandmother's theory of evolution: Symbiotic mergers, not hostile take-overs.

Sisters, as lesbians, we are not always brilliant at achieving symbiotic mergers with each other, much less other species. We lesbians have a tendency toward unhealthy-for-both-merging-identity mergers, or else we are known for attempting mergers—like in collectives—that have a way of blowing up in our faces. We are not immune to the forces of patriarchy, and certainly we do our share of good-old-fashioned patriarchal dominance and submission… which is pretty much the universal model for interacting with the environment… except for indigenous cultures following traditional ways. Where we do shine is in the arena of rugged individualism.

And that's why we're talking about this today. So now, we're going to peek into Margulis' book and look at some examples, that maybe we can learn from. In explaining to the lay person how symbiosis works, Margulis uses the example of lichen. Lichen is a combination of two organisms living in a mutually beneficial arrangement. Most of the lichen is composed of fungal filaments, but among these filaments are green algal cells. Fungus and algae, sisters. Two completely different organisms, like you and your partner.

Now, fungus will die if it's covered in water, but algae will thrive. On the other hand, if there isn't enough sunlight to power up green algae's photosynthesis, or food-making, then it will die out. The fungus doesn't need the sun to survive. So you can see how, without each other, these plants have serious vulnerabilities: need for air and need for sun. But look what happens when they join forces to become lichen. The algae gains a structure that enables it to live on land, and the fungus benefits from the food-making capacity of the algae. And now, scientists are finding that there may even be a third participant, possibly some form of bacteria.

Anyway... moving to mammals for her examples of symbiosis, Margulis describes the cow as a fifty-gallon fermentation vat. The cow does not digest the grass it eats. The grass is digested by the micro-organisms that are growing—yes, symbiotically—inside its gut. The micro-organisms get their meals delivered by the cow, while the cow gets the benefits of the nutrients that are released when the micro-organisms digest the grass.

Which brings us to the human colon. Yes, sisters... for the sake of the planet, let us consider the mighty colon.

The colon is host to the bacteria that constitute the largest percentage of the dry weight of the human body. That right there is a pretty staggering thought, but we need to keep moving. On the planet, there are at least 17 families of bacteria with 50 different genera. Within this are hundreds of species and subspecies. We each host somewhere between 400-500 different species and subspecies inside our bodies. And whether we like it or not, these bacteria constitute a de facto Lower GI Tract Tenants' Association. When we are not eating with proper symbiotic respect for the needs of the bacteria in our gut, they die out or the more harmful ones proliferate, and we find, like most slumlords, that lowlife tenants have a way of making their problems into problems for the landlords.

Unhappy colon bacteria can form pockets of resistance, trash the place, or stage a sit-down strike.

Now it's not my focus today to talk about the digestive system. I just want to point out that it evolved, not by survival of the most rugged, self-sufficient gut that can digest all kinds of crap because it's so damn tough... but it evolved through a very delicate balance, a rich symbiosis of relationships with all kinds of colonies of other living beings that take up habitation there. We feed them and in exchange, they aid in digestion for us. If we eat crap they can't digest, they die and the food is not digested and we don't absorb nutrients from it. Bacteria. Tenants. Symbiosis.

And as below, so above. What does that mean? As the colon goes, so goes the planet. We survive individually the best when we are in rich, delicately balanced symbiotic mergers with other humans and also other forms of life and also with the rocks and the weather and the rivers and the ocean. We are good to them and they are good to us.

As a planet and as individuals we have to take Saint Margulis' Gaia Concept very seriously. We have to move away from "natural selection"... which is kind of a contradiction in terms. Remember what it felt like when kids got to pick their teams in middle school? Yeah, not good. Definitely not symbiotic. The whole notion of selection seems predicated on selfishness and grandiosity. Nothing natural about it. So let's move from natural selection to the Gaia Concept. Symbiotic Merger. This is a radical, radical rerouting of our synapses.

Now, sisters, I know that there are a lot of us who grasp the importance of recycling and boycotting Monsanto and cutting greenhouse emissions, but who are not so keen to see the importance of symbiosis in our personal relationships. Many of us are morbidly attached to toxic levels of self-sufficiency. Toxic because that's just what they are. They put us outside symbiotic systems that support the planet. We can isolate ourselves in our so-called self-sufficiency and even glory in that. We can hoard. We can lie to ourselves. We can think we're doing fine, when we are actually heading over a cliff of total breakdown and dependency. We can feel superior. We can be judgmental about others who are not so self-sufficient.

And all our mighty systems of independence can come tumbling down with something as tiny as the bite of tick so small we can hardly see it. Ask anyone who has contracted Lyme disease.

Sister Carolyn speaks with authority here, because she used to take pride in the fact she never asked for help. She used to feel that was a good thing. She took care of herself... except of course for those multiple occasions when she would have some kind of breakdown from an accumulation of unmet and usually unconscious needs. And these breakdowns would be experienced as events outside her control, and as soon as she was on her feet again, she would go back to the belief she was self-sufficient... at least, until the next breakdown.

And what about her friends? Well, when Sister Carolyn had a breakdown or a meltdown, they didn't have a lot of options. They either showed up because they cared, or else they had to kind of abandon her. Pretty much black-and-white, on-the-bus or off-the-bus. Not given a lot of options or advance warnings. In fact, my breakdowns were kind of a squeeze play, forcing other people to pick up the pieces.

And then I learned that asking for help early and often was a good thing. I learned that when I asked for help early, I had lots of options, because the problem wasn't that urgent or that overwhelming. And because I was asking for help often, I needed to get a pretty large roster of folks I could contact, so I wouldn't have to burn out any one person. This was a really good thing, because it meant no one person felt they had to show up. It made it so that anyone I reached out to could say "no" pretty comfortably, because I wasn't in crisis and I could tell them that I actually had a list of other folks I could contact if this wasn't a good time or wouldn't work for them. Amazingly, Sister Carolyn stopped having breakdowns and meltdowns. She started having good days and bad days instead. And that has proven to be a symbiotic thing for all involved.

But here's the thing. Nobody can meet all her own needs all the time. And if we think we can, what is actually happening is that we are building up a store of unmet needs in the sub-basement of our subconscious. The more we tell ourselves we are being self-sufficient, the more we are stuffing our needs, and one day they are going to reach some kind of critical mass and explode, and that's when we have the breakdown.

And here's another thing. When the needs are all subterranean like that, we actually are desperate. We are. Doesn't matter how competent we look. We are actually desperate. As Henry

David Thoreau would say, we areliving lives of quiet desperation. And while I'm quoting American writers, here's Robert Lewis Stevenson: "Sooner or later everyone sits down to a banquet of consequences." Or as poet Saint Judy Grahn said, "All the chickens come home to roost. All of them." And they do and they will, sisters. All of them.

And that desperation can suck our friends dry. We've probably all dated or worked for folks who are desperate but don't know it. They don't have normal interactions with us. They are scavenging the conversation. They are siphoning us emotionally. They might try to hypnotize or paralyze us so they can feed on our life force, our vital energy... anything they might be able to use to feed all those unmet needs.

And, sisters, they can't help it anymore than we can help it if we are loaded with unmet needs. The only way to be accountable is be sure we don't have this basement of unmet needs when we come to the table of human interactions. If we have a process in place for identifying and meeting these needs before they pile up, then we don't have to ambush folks with our multiple breakdowns and crises. We don't have to take our friends hostage.

Here's the thing with toxic self-sufficiency. It's a kind of *folie de deux*. *Folie de deux* is a French term meaning "madness of two." It happens when two people transmit delusional beliefs back and forth. Like one person says, "I'm the Queen of France." And the other bows and says, "Indeed you are, Your Highness." *Folie de deux.* I think that *folie de deux* can happen between a person and her self-sufficiency. She says, "Hey, I'm self-sufficient, aren't I?" and her self-sufficiency looks at her checkbook, or her job, or her homegrown vegetables and says, "You sure are." And then she says, "So I don't need anything from anyone, do I?" and her self-sufficiency says, "No, you sure don't. And you're better off that way, because other people may abandon you." And so this goes on back and forth... the dyke and her self-sufficiency... congratulating each other on their great wisdom in not needing anyone else. And, sisters, this is a *folie de deux.* Why? Because the self-sufficiency is a myth that makes a lot of assumptions. Assumptions like, "my job will last forever" or "my health will last forever" or "the economy is going to be strong and a dollar today will buy the same thing in a year or ten years." If we are deeply invested in the myth of our self-sufficiency, we are making all kinds of false assumptions all the time.

The fact of the matter is this: Our self-sufficiency may collapse any time. Like I said... all it takes is a tick bite, or an uninsured fire, or a business based on working with a partner who up and leaves. Think about all those folks in 2008, who had been counting on their 401(k) account for their retirement.

Understanding that the world is an unsafe place is uncomfortable. People would much rather upload a myth about self-sufficiency than really accept that there are huge factors that can impact our welfare over which we have ZERO control. But that's the truth. And if we learn to embrace our lack of security, we can actually achieve some level of security around that. We can develop a wide network of symbiotic relationships that will buffer us from all kinds of weird catastrophes... And this, sisters, is FAR better than our misguided faith in our toxic self-sufficiency.

The most truly self-sufficient people understand that self-sufficiency is a myth.

Sister Carolyn has known two people in her life who took great pride in living off the grid and not needing anyone for anything. And one of them was found in a coma in his cabin up in the mountains of Colorado, had to be flown back to his family in Maryland, and ended his life with a barrage of arguably toxic medical treatments over which he had no control at all... treatments which represented the antithesis of his entire philosophy of living.

The other friend had spent her life trying to escape from the terrible nightmare of her childhood vulnerabilities. She had set about becoming so independent she wouldn't need anybody or anything. But then, at midlife, these nightmares caught up to her all of a sudden in the form of Complex PTSD, which was misdiagnosed (as it often is), and she ended up dependent on a subsidized medical system which provided miserable health care... setting her up for addiction to a slew of psychotropic drugs which rendered her too fatigued to maintain her farm which led rapidly to suicidal ideation and eventual death.

And I had a third lesbian friend who had spent her life building her own businesses and making sure she was in control of every aspect of her life. For years, she had paid into insurance for long-term health care, and when she was old, she picked out one of the most expensive assisted living communities. But she could not control the homophobia of the staff and residents in this community. Sadly, it turned out that quality of life she had sought so rigorously was not solely dependent on how much money she had.

It sucks that so many of us learned not to trust people. And it sucks that self-sufficiency doesn't really work. It really does. We should be able to control things by controlling things. And I have tried, sisters. I have tried. But it just does not work. You know it. I know it. It doesn't work.

Let us take a moment to honor the words of Saint Julia Penelope:

> "I have learned that when I believed myself to be most 'in control' of my mind, my body, my life, I was least 'in control.' When I would have declared, and believed, that I was 'on top' of relationships and events in my life, I was most the victim of my past and the consequences of my experiences. Realizing this in my own life, I have come to believe that the most damaging idea we've learned from our culture is the equation of power with control, and its corollary, the identification of control with autonomy and independence"

This requires a big shift for us as individuals. And it's a huge shift for the planet. But here in the US, our self-sufficiency has been based on oil… and we are discovering that we are alarmingly vulnerable because of that. We have had lower oil prices than other countries for decades, and congratulated ourselves on our political leverage in achieving that. But other countries with those more realistic oil prices have been busily converting to wind and solar technologies, and we are waking up to see that we have been the suckers, not they. We have to lie to ourselves about so many things in order to pretend that we are a self-sufficient nation.

So... big shifts for all of us. The whole Gaia Concept, this symbiotic merger model. It's the polar opposite of competition, of survival of the fittest. But here is the good news, sisters: Your colon gets it. Your colon lives it. Every time you expel methane gas in a fart, you can know that you are experiencing the blessing of symbiotic merger... in those hosts of friendly bacteria who get free groceries in exchange for digesting them. I believe that we can learn to be as smart as our colons. I do. I believe we can. We just need to learn to wrap our heads around our colon... which is the opposite of having our heads up our asses... which is what toxic self-sufficiency is all about.

Blessed be!

Sermon on Complex PTSD

All right now sisters, listen up. We're talking about something really, really important today. We're talking about Complex PTSD. That's Complex Post Traumatic Stress Disorder. Why is it so important? Because a boatload of lesbians have it, and a boatload of lesbians don't know they have it... sometimes because they have been misdiagnosed. If they don't know they have it, they can go through a lot of suffering and confusion that they don't need to. And if they are misdiagnosed, they can die. That's right. Just happened to a good friend of mine.

If you have Complex PTSD and you are misdiagnosed, you can die. She killed herself. Complex PTSD is frequently misdiagnosed as borderline personality, or depression, or a whole range of other things, and it is often treated in ways that make it much worse. So we are going to be looking at Complex PTSD today and what it is and what it is not. And we are going to look at it all kinds of ways... not just psychologically, but politically and socially and lesbianically. And we are going to weave it back into the web, and we are going to weave our sisters who have it back into a giant network of understanding. Because, sisters, we cannot afford to lose each other. None of us. I mean it.

And Complex PTSD is something different. Not to be confused with that whole host of other diagnoses for what is often explained as "broken brains" to patients. Don't get me started. Complex PTSD is actually the opposite. It's a diagnosis for a brain that is operating very, very well, thank you. Too well, maybe.

What do I mean?

Well, lets say you grew up on Mars. Whole other planet. Whole other environment. Whole other customs. Whole other culture. Whole other survival needs. That's the key. I'm going to say that again: Whole other survival needs. Like maybe water. Like where is it, how to get it, who has it, how to keep it. Like maybe an entire language around the scarcity of water, adaptations to that scarcity, terrors around the ongoing threat of not having enough... and so on. Perhaps a preoccupation with water that might look like an obsession to a culture that has water on demand in every faucet in the house.

So if you came from Mars, grew up on Mars, and then moved to earth, you would have to do a lot of reprogramming... a lot of relearning... based on the culture here. That vigilance-about-water thing that kept you alive as a child is going to cause you problems here. First off, folks aren't going to understand your "obsession." It's going to scare them or annoy them. You're going to act or seem inappropriate in a lot of situations. Folks are going to back off. So now you're going to have the issues that people have who are unable to make connections with other people. And this might cause you to isolate, which causes a host of other adaptations that will make it even harder to connect. And so on and so on. Not a damn thing wrong with your brain. It adapted brilliantly to conditions on Mars. In fact it learned how to survive on Mars so well, it's having a tough time letting go of those lessons that were so powerfully and maybe even traumatically reinforced. Maybe you saw people die on Mars because they were careless with water, or too generous with it. What folks might call "trust issues" could just be that you learned too well. No "broken brain" here at all. But a brain that needs to unlearn and reprogram. Okay. That's the first analogy.

Second analogy. Let's take a black eye. Let's say you got hit in the eye with a wild softball pitch. But let's say, for whatever crazy reason, the doctor treating you does not know that. In fact, let's say that the doctor treating you has a very, very limited practice and does not know anything about people getting hit with objects in the face. This doctor would note the swelling, the blue color of the skin around the socket, the throbbing pain, the bloodshot eye. Let's say she specializes in diseases of the eye and has very little experience in other areas of medicine.

You know what? She might conclude that you had a disease of the eye. And a pretty scary one. It's turning color, it's swelling... I don't know—will it eat up your whole head? Will it turn orange tomorrow? And the bloodshot eye... are you going blind? She might put you through a bazillion tests that just scare her even more because she can't find a cause in a microscope or an x-ray. She might recommend that you wrap your whole head tightly so that the swelling won't eat your whole head. She might inject you with skin-colored dye so the blue skin is less blue. See where I'm going with this? And she might diagnose a diseased eye. If you remembered that your mom once had a shiner like yours, she might put down that it was hereditary... which might send the doctor down a whole path of genetic mapping, searching for the black-eye gene.

The truth of the matter, of course, is that this is a perfectly healthy eye, doing what perfectly healthy eyes do when they have sustained an impact injury. And all of the things happening are a result of either the trauma to the tissue or the body's attempt to heal the damage. Process. There is a PROCESS going on. A healthy process that just happens to look kind of weird and scary.

Okay, so Mars and black eyes. What does this have to do with Complex PTSD? Well, what is Complex PTSD? All right... here's a definition: *"Complex post-traumatic stress disorder (C-PTSD) is a psychological injury that results from protracted exposure to prolonged social and/or interpersonal trauma in the context of either captivity or entrapment (a situation lacking a viable escape route for the victim), which results in the lack or loss of control, helplessness, and deformations of identity and sense of self."*

Okay, that's a mouthful. Let's break it down, and, more specifically, let's break it down in specific lesbian terms. It's a *"psychological injury..."* Okay. It's *not* a brain disease. It's a psychological injury. *"Protracted exposure to a prolonged social and/or interpersonal trauma..."* Okay, like, say homophobia? Like socially being taught you're going to hell, or that who you are is going to cause you to get the shit beat out of you on the playground every day, or that you can never marry, never have the career you wanted, and so on and so on...? And the *"interpersonal trauma..."* Well, the

104

playground thing, but also rejection by family and/or friends. And this happens in a context of either *"captivity or entrapment"*... which is defined as a situation *"lacking a viable escape route."* Well, lesbians historically would flee to San Francisco, or before that, Greenwich Village. Prior to the 1950's witch-hunts, we would seek jobs with the federal government. But really, there was no escape route for homophobia. And the results? *"Lack or loss of control, helplessness, and deformations of identity and sense of self."* What does it mean to have to deny who you are in order to take care of yourself? When forced to hide one's identity, how can one avoid internalizing a sense of shame about that identity? And so on...

And, there's something else: child sexual abuse. Many lesbians, on top of the protracted exposure to prolonged homophobia, have had to deal with growing up with violence in the home and/or sexual abuse. Protracted exposure to prolonged violence, terror, threat of violence in a context of captivity or entrapment and having no escape route. Parents have near-absolute control over their children... Captivity is a word that, sadly, describes the experience of many children. That captivity can be with or without the entrapment of brainwashing... being taught that the abuse is normal, or deserved. Some children learn that they have an obligation to submit sexually, or that the violence is a form of discipline. And so on. With what result? *"Lack and loss of control, helplessness, and deformations of identity and sense of self."*

And a note on these "deformations"... Sometimes they protect a child. Believing that one is bad holds out the hope that one can someday change and not be deserving of the abuse. Believing that one's parents are violent and irrational monsters can be overwhelming to the developing ego. A belief that gives the victim any sense of control will often be adopted as a survival tactic. Life on Mars. And also the black eye to the brain. BUT NOTHING ORGANICALLY wrong with the brain. In fact, the brain of a tortured captive may be functioning on overdrive to save the victim's life.

But... here we are twenty or thirty years later. And here is a lesbian, who has had a pretty strong young adulthood... maybe she's even a super-achiever. But now, suddenly, she is having panic attacks. A lot of them, seemingly coming from nowhere. They don't appear to be related to what's going on. In fact, her life may be the best it's ever been. Or maybe she has depression showing up. Debilitating depression... loss of interest in her life, all that stuff. Crying uncontrollably in the middle of the day for no discernable reason. Maybe even thinking of suicide.

Before the doctors get out all their books on "broken brains" and hereditary mental illness and bad-science theories about brains that have low levels of this and that... which, by the way, have NEVER been measured. (You can't measure levels of substances inside a working brain without killing the patient. Duh.) Anyway, before they go down that road, what about looking for trauma... the life on Mars, the softball in the face/psyche?

Well... if they did that, they might just come up with a diagnosis of Complex PTSD. And Complex PTSD has a whole different treatment protocol from the so-called "broken-brain" diagnoses. Misdiagnosing Complex PTSD can and often does cause huge suffering, and misprescribed medications counterindicated for Complex PTSD can result in a range of debilitating side effects often serious enough to qualify the patient for disability. These misdiagnoses can derail the body's natural attempts to heal. Kind of like shooting the "normal-color" dye into the black eye tissue. The process of healing from a black eye may be tough to watch... the swelling, the bloodshot eye, the wild colors of the skin, as it goes from blue to yellow. But all that scary and seemingly unnatural appearance is exactly what the body needs to do. Trying to make that black-eye look normal immediately is not going to help and is likely to cause all kinds of other problems. Focusing on "let's get this back to a normal appearance" may actually be about not respecting and honoring a difficult internal process.

This is why it is so important for lesbians to take responsibility for understanding Complex PTSD. If there has been prolonged trauma in the lesbian's history, this should be the first diagnosis to be considered. Sadly, it can be the last. Why? Because it's not yet in the *Diagnostic and Statistical Manual of Mental Disorders*, (*DSM*) which is the official manual for diagnosing psychological disorders... The *DSM* is the book that standardizes diagnoses, and it's the book that qualifies a condition for insurance coverage. Very powerful, the *DSM*.

Here at the Lesbian Tent Revival, we call it the *Diabolically Strategic Manual* of patriarchy that masquerades as hard science, when in fact, it frequently simply mirrors the political and social mores of the time. For instance, homosexuality used to be in there. Frigidity still is. It has another fancier name, but that's what it is. Which most of us lesbians understand to be "Male Ignorance About Women's Bodies Syndrome" or "Male Selfishness Syndrome." I could go on. I really could. Multiple sclerosis used to be considered a form of hysteria… that is, a form of mental illness. Chronic Fatigue Syndrome (ME/CFS) and Lyme disease are still too often treated as if they are psychosomatic, that is, *"caused or aggravated by a mental factor like stress or internal conflict."* Regular PTSD, Post-Traumatic Stress Disorder from a single event like a car accident or an assault is in the *DSM*… but not Complex PTSD, which is common with survivors of domestic violence and/or child sexual abuse, which is why the diagnosis can be missed.

Insurance will pay for treatment for regular PTSD (car accident,) but it will not cover the patient who is suffering acutely from the aftermath of decades of terrorism in her own home. The therapist treating that woman must find another diagnosis, usually a "broken brain" one, in order to have insurance cover the therapy.

ANYWAY… the whole issue of PTSD has been a hot potato, and Complex PTSD is the thermonuclear potato. PTSD was first identified among veterans coming back from Vietnam in the 1970's. Not like soldiers haven't had PTSD until then. It was just called "shell shock," "battle fatigue," and other vague euphemisms. Until Vietnam, the condition was not identified as a specific syndrome, and there was no standardized protocol for treating it… other than furlough or bed rest.

Needless to say, the military is not a fan of PTSD, now that it has become an official diagnosis. The Veteran's Administration has to treat it. And that's expensive. In recent years, so many veterans were turning up with PTSD, they started a system where soldiers who were leaving the service were asked if they had it, and if they said yes, they were kept on for weeks of so-called "evaluation." Well, obviously anyone suffering from PTSD wants to get the hell home ASAP... and so there was intense pressure on the most vulnerable to deny the presence of the condition. And then, too, there is a kind of machismo in military culture... PTSD is for those who "can't take it"... who aren't "man enough" to witness slaughter of civilians, etc., etc.

Anyway... PTSD is very different from Complex PTSD. Folks diagnosed with PTSD are folks surviving serious car accidents, victims of one-time assaults, soldiers, folks who have been involved in short-term hostage scenarios. What is different is that they don't have the *"protracted exposure to prolonged social and/or interpersonal trauma in the context of either captivity or entrapment...a situation lacking a viable escape route for the victim."* You could say, folks suffering from PTSD didn't grow up on Mars. They have a sense of functional identity and safety to which they can return once they work through the trauma. The person with Complex PTSD has to rebuild and reprogram a lot more, because they have been living for so long with the trauma response. If they were born into and raised in homes with domestic violence, they never developed a functional identity or sense of safety. You can't return to something you never had.

ANYWAY… back to the very, very recent history of PTSD as an official diagnosis. Okay, so it was discovered with Vietnam vets, but then folks working in the field of domestic violence started noticing something. They started noticing that the victims of domestic violence, especially children, and especially children with sexual abuse histories, were exhibiting symptoms very similar to those of returning prisoners-of-war. Wow. And why wouldn't they? They had spent years living in captivity, with threats and terror, and they had developed *"lack or loss of control, helplessness, and deformations of identity and sense of self."*

This connection broke a huge taboo… Suddenly people were looking at the patriarchal nuclear family and beginning to frame it as a war zone, where wives, girlfriends, and children were in positions analogous to prisoners-of-war. Wow. This was huge. So much easier to talk about "crazy women" and give them pills or lock them up. This diagnosis meant looking at a crime and identifying the perpetrators. And it also meant noticing that it was an epidemic. (And a side note here: Yes, women can be perpetrators of domestic terrorism, and men and boys can be the victims. Males can certainly develop Complex PTSD. It's not my intention to trivialize their situation, but I am speaking specifically to lesbians here, and I am also aware that the percentage of defendents in domestic violence cases is over 90% male.)

Anyway, a full integration of the magnitude of Complex PTSD would require a complete paradigm shift in the culture… one that was feminist and focused on the safety of women and the developmental needs of the child. In fact, our

110

culture is moving in the opposite direction about as fast as it can, as more and more folks have to work outside the home more and more hours, and the kids just have to suck it up. The pornographizing of the culture is advancing, desensitizing children to sexual abuses and rendering them more vulnerable and perpetrators less accountable. And of course, as the economy tanks, social services are drying up… and, as noted before, Complex PTSD requires a paradigm shift in the delivery of health care, too… which is why it's not in the *DSM* yet.

So… let's look at the treatment for Complex PTSD.

It has been suggested that treatment for C-PTSD should differ from treatment for PTSD by focusing on problems that cause more functional impairment than the PTSD symptoms.

Okay… so here are some of the symptoms of Complex PTSD. This is called the "adult symptom cluster."

- *Difficulties regulating emotions, including symptoms such as persistent sadness, suicidal thoughts, explosive anger, or covert anger.* Triggers, sisters. We often have things that trigger us, things that are consciously or unconsciously associated with abuses from the past

- *Variations in consciousness, such as forgetting traumatic events (i.e., psychogenic amnesia), reliving traumatic events, or having episodes of dissociation (during which one feels detached from one's mental processes or body).* And here I want to note that

111

historically lesbians have had to dissociate from our lesbian truths and our lesbian identities to survive.

- *Changes in self-perception, such as a chronic and pervasive sense of helplessness, shame, guilt, stigma, and a sense of being completely different from other human beings.* Again, being lesbian.

- *Varied changes in the perception of the perpetrator, such as attributing total power to the perpetrator or becoming preoccupied with the relationship to the perpetrator, including a preoccupation with revenge.*

- *Alterations in relations with others, including isolation, distrust, or a repeated search for a rescuer.*

- *Loss of, or changes in, one's system of meanings, which may include a loss of sustaining faith or a sense of hopelessness and despair.* This can be about our spirituality, sisters. When terrible and unfair things happen, we can find it difficult to find joy in anything, and certainly some of our old-fashioned ideas about God or the Goddess can be called—and rightly so— into question. This is a serious business, sisters. Because living with an overwhelming sense of atrocity makes for a life not worth living.

So how do you treat Complex PTSD? Well, there are six suggested core components of treatment. What are they?

- Safety

- Self-regulation
- Self-reflective information processing... like the kind of radical thinking that goes on at the Lesbian Tent Revival.
- Integration of traumatic experiences
- Relational engagement, which is fancy talk for being in relationships with folks
- Positive affect enhancement

Sisters, there are medications that can temporarily calm an anxiety attack, and it's important to note that the most common one lists depression as a side effect. Sisters, read the side effects of the drugs you take! Is it worth trading transitory panic attacks for chronic depression? And yes, there are more pills for depression, and it's important to note that 80% of folks taking anti-depressants long term will morph into folks with bi-polar disorder. Again, is it worth it? And yes, there are meds for bi-polar, and it's important to note that taking meds for anxiety, depression, and for mood-stabilizing can lead to sleep disorders. And, yes, there are meds for that. And these are highly addictive.

And it's important to note that nobody... NOBODY knows what these meds do in combination with each other, but that the US government has accepted that, in combination, they can result in disability, because it will approve disability claims from folks just from the documentation of the prescriptions. Combining these drugs can result in overwhelming fatigue, fatigue so great that a person cannot work. Again, is it worth it? It is also important to note that anti-depressants can cause suicidal thinking. They have to print a "black box" label (highest level) warning now about how this is true for young people. But it can also be true for adults. That warning is in the list of side effects. It also bears noting that many of these drugs are highly addictive, and that patients are not always given accurate information about that.

And sisters, if you are considering taking these, it might be helpful to do a little research on how the psychotropic drugs were discovered. In fact, many of them were discovered accidentally. Many of them came out of World War II, when there was a big push to discover new antibiotics. Along the way, researchers began to notice that some of these substances made people super happy or calmed people down, et cetera. You might want to check out the book *Anatomy of an Epidemic*, which has a subtitle: *Magic Bullets, Psychiatric Drugs, and the Astonishing Rise of Mental Illness in America*. It's written by an insider in the pharmaceutical industry. Quite an eye-opener.

Anyway... long-term prescriptions are not the protocol for Complex PTSD. In fact, they are counter-indicated. I'm going to read that list again of what people need for healing if we have Complex PTSD:

> Safety
> Self-regulation
> Self-reflective information processing
> Traumatic experiences integration
> Relational engagement
> Positive affect enhancement

As you can tell, these are not take-a-pill or have-a-procedure items. These are huge "step-up-and-take-responsibility-for-your-life" things. These are "get-a-healing-community-around-you" things. These are "get-some-trusted-role-models-for-feedback" things. This is a list of tremendous changes that can't be made with a leap into a new job, or a new neighborhood, or a new relationship. These are the kinds of changes that require slow, small alterations in attitudes and behaviors which, over time, will culminate in integration and transformation.

There are two things that trauma does: It alienates us from our fellow human beings and it destroys our systems of meaning-slash-faith because, "How the hell could such an awful thing have happened?" Healing requires restoration of a sense of belonging to a community and it also requires a rebuilding of a system of meaning and /or faith.

So… Complex PTSD. Identified by feminist therapist Judith Hermann and first described in 1992 in her book *Trauma & Recovery: The Aftermath of Violence—from Domestic Abuse to Political Terror.* Sisters, that's the Bible for Complex PTSD. Read it. Share it. There is a war on in the field of mental health. As lesbians, we need to be addiction literate and also trauma literate, because so many of our sisters experience both. We need to know what we are seeing. We need to know how to support each other. We need to understand what is affecting us and we need to understand what we need to heal.

Blessed be.

Sermon on Stockholm Syndrome

Sisters… many years ago, before everyone's identities were considered so fluid you couldn't talk about them, there was a lesbian who set about publishing a collection of essays in response to the question, "What is a lesbian?" Now, this collection never did get published, but it did prompt Sister Carolyn to consider seriously how to answer that question.

And what I answered it with was another question. Which is a handy trick in the world of Patriarchal Universal Discourse. You know, "PUD." PUD was discovered and named by Sister Julia Penelope who was one of the most dazzlingly brilliant synapsers among the Sisterhood of the Sacred Synapse… which is to say radically thinking lesbians. She discovered PUD, and a whole lot of other things that are worth studying up on… ANYWAY… in PUD the questions they put to women in general, and to lesbians in particular, are often framed in such a way that no matter how you answer them, you end up erasing your own reality. So answering a question with a question is not a bad thing. It's a way to shift the paradigm—and a paradigm is a model of reality—it's a way of shifting that model of reality back to your home court. So you can have the home court advantage. In the words of Malcolm X, "Don't struggle only within the ground rules that the people you are struggling against laid down."

All right, so I was asked to write something that would answer the question, "What is a lesbian?" and the more I thought

116

about it, the more it just seemed to me that it was the wrong question to be asking.

And I think that Sister Judy Grahn also thought that way, because she wrote this poem called "A History of Lesbianism" that pretty much says, "that's not the question." So, I'm going to take a little minute here and recite these words of Ms. Grahn... this is from *Edward the Dyke and Other Poems*... which, by the way, when queer folks try to insist that lesbians did not deal with intersectionality of oppressions until postmodernism came along... you just send them to that collection and tell them to read, "A Woman Is Talking to Death," which has more intersections than a map of Manhattan.

ANYWAY... This is Grahn's "A History of Lesbianism," and you can go to Youtube and hear her read it herself...

> The subject of lesbianism
> is very ordinary; it's the question
> of male domination that makes everybody
> angry.

Now, getting back to that question about "What is a lesbian?"... Here Sister Grahn tells us. The whole subject is very ordinary. And the dictionary tells us that "ordinary" means "normal and commonplace." Lesbianism is very normal and commonplace. So why is it that the world has treated us like something so dangerous we can't be allowed to exist, and STILL even with all the hoopla around marriage equality and so on... STILL we are not represented with any accuracy or even very much frequency in the media? So anyway... if lesbianism is so normal and commonplace, why is it that folks can't seem to wrap their heads around who we are, and want to ask, " What is a lesbian?" Or even "*Why* is a lesbian?"

And Sister Grahn explains that, too. And she explains it so clearly and so simply that folks are just hell-bent to ignore or misunderstand her, which is what they do when you are absolutely clear. And I learned that at Sister Andrea Dworkin's memorial service in New York. There was a speaker and I regret that I did not note the name of the speaker, but she said that "Andrea was always clear, and because she was always clear, she was always misunderstood. Andrea was always fierce, and because of this, she was always vulnerable."

ANYWAY... Sister Grahn explains why lesbians are considered such an upsetting phenomenon when, in fact, lesbianism is very ordinary. She tells us *"it's the question/ of male domination that makes everybody/ angry."*

I'm going to say that again, in case there is any lesbian here today having any confusion about the roots her oppression... which is to say, who is confused about why she can feel crazy or depressed or sick or bad or crazy or wrong: "It's the question of male domination that makes everybody angry."

Well... okay... but why does this make people treat lesbians like we are some kind of outlaws? Why are we the target if it's male domination that makes everyone so angry?

Okay and now I'm going to wend my way back to the original subject of this sermon, which was how I responded when I was asked to write an essay answering the question, "What is a lesbian?"

And how did I answer it? I answered it with: "Lesbians are just women. The real question is what is a heterosexual woman?"

Because in the PUD, or Patriarchal Universal Discourse, the heterosexual woman is considered the norm, and the lesbian has been framed as the one with the problem, or the deviance, or the kink, or the childhood gone wrong. The updated version of this is that heterosexual women are normal, and now so are lesbians. Which is a way of framing identity that still protects the fact that male domination is a universal phenomenon and that, because of this, lesbianism BY DEFINITION is a site of resistance as well as a strategy for liberation.

Yeah. And that's the reason why all this anger about male domination gets aimed at us.

The real question is "What is a straight woman?"

Let's ask the questions that put us at the center of our own reality. Instead of us having to explain ourselves, how about our straight sisters having to explain themselves?

Now, sisters. I know… I know… This is a painful subject. Lots of emotions around it. Lots of heat… Why? Because "the question of male domination makes everybody angry." So let's just breathe into it.

Now, we know that there is a lot of child abuse. We know that statistically one out of five girls are sexually abused before eighteen and one out of twenty boys. That's a boatload of abuse. And we know that 95% of the perpetrators are men.

We know something else. We know that in order to colonize a nation, the colonizers only need to terrorize 15% of the population. So, if we think about the terrorizing and the violation of children, we've got 20% of girls. That's 5% more than than is needed to colonize the entire female population.

And we know something else. We know that there is something called Stockholm Syndrome, and that this is a very real thing. What is Stockholm Syndrome? It is defined as a psychological phenomenon in which hostages express empathy and sympathy and have positive feelings toward their captors, sometimes to the point of defending them. Empathy and sympathy and POSITIVE FEELINGS toward their captors... sometimes to the point of defending them.

According to statistics from the FBI's Hostage Barricade Database System, 8% of all hostage situation victims show signs of Stockholm Syndrome... close to one tenth. But we know that you don't need a formal hostage situation like a bank hold-up to develop this syndrome.

The definition of a hostage is "a person seized or held as security for the fulfillment of a condition." A condition like marriage. Or paying the bills that keep a roof over your children's head. Here is another description of Stockholm Syndrome from the Freebase online database:

> *Stockholm Syndrome can be seen as a form of traumatic bonding, which does not necessarily require a hostage scenario, but which describes "strong emotional ties that develop between two persons where one person intermittently harasses, beats, threatens, abuses, or intimidates the other."*

In other words, this could develop in a home with an abusive father figure, or a school with an abusive teacher, or coach… or a boss. Lots of different ways this could develop.

Now, why on earth would a person bond with their captor or their abuser?

Let's go back to the fact that humans are animals. We all keep forgetting that. Like the planet is populated by animals and humans. Which is an easy mistake, because we tend to kill or violate all the other species on the planet, which is something none of the other species do. But human are still animals. And we have animal biology and animal behaviors that have more or less evolved. Now it might be nice if that biology and those behaviors had evolved for the purpose of our individual self-realization and pursuit of happiness… but if that had been the case, it's likely none of us would have been here. Most likely, we would have been wiped out back with the dinosaurs.

We are here, because our biology and our behaviors evolved with one goal in mind: Survival of the gene pool. That meant

121

females reproducing early and often and males inseminating early and often. In the genetic derby, aggression and domination gave males an advantage. What about the females? Ongoing aggression and domination are not the skills to see a female through a long gestation and the years of child-rearing necessary for the higher primates. Stockholm Syndrome actually gives the female an evolutionary edge. She's going to bond with the most violent male in the tribe. This can provide protection from other males... and we know that in the gorilla family, alpha males do kill the offspring of other males... again a form of natural selection.

In fact, a female gorilla whose infant is torn from her arms and killed by a male in a display of dominance has been observed to *spontaneously and instantaneously* bond with that murderous male. Why? Because this serves the survival of the gene pool. She survives, and she will mate with a male even stronger and more aggressive than her previous mate, and as a result of that coupling, she may produce offspring who will inherit the superior alpha qualities of the male, as well as the mother's highly developed Stockholm Syndrome, or genetic predisposition toward instantaneous, high-level, dissociative trauma bonding. All good for survival of the gene pool.

The Freebase database has a Freudian take on this subject:

> *One commonly used hypothesis to explain the effect of Stockholm syndrome is based on Freudian theory. It suggests that the bonding is the individual's response to trauma in becoming a victim. Identifying with the aggressor is one way that the ego defends itself. When a victim believes the same values as the aggressor, they*

cease to be a threat. Battered-person syndrome is an example of activating the capture–bonding psychological mechanism, as are military basic training and fraternity bonding by hazing.

Now in the sermon about the Real L-Words we talked quite a bit about the chemistry of so-called romance—an unromantic subject if ever there was one!—and how the chemicals in our brain can trick us into falling in love with all kinds of folks who will make our lives miserable. Why? Because the focus of the hard-wired brain is on the mating, on the survival of the gene pool... not on our individual fulfillment.

We have to outsmart our biology, and a lot of the biology that needs outsmarting—in fact, most of it—is between our ears. And that can be tough. Because when your brain is telling you something, it can be very tough to argue with it. I mean, with what are you going to do the arguing? Your brain? So one half of your brain is going to take on the other half?

Actually, that's exactly what we need to do. We build alternative synapses. We build a helicopter in our brain to lift us right out of the amygdala, which is the primitive brain, so we can look down on all that mental wiring that is about survival of the gene pool. And then, from this enlightened position, we can make a CHOICE. Because the survival of the gene pool is no longer the issue. We humans have, in fact, outnumbered and overrun the damn planet to such a degree that we have become a danger to ourselves.

What does it take to build that helicopter? What does it take for the fish to know it's wet? It takes an experience of dry land. Or it takes a colossal act of faith on the part of the fish to believe that there is another environment, another whole way of living and moving that is different from the one it knows. Or maybe it takes a messenger who has seen that other world and who can report back to us about it.

Sisters, lesbian-feminist community, lesbian-feminist culture is that helicopter… that way out of the PUD, the Patriarchal Universal Discourse. Lesbian-feminist culture can lift us out of that gene-pool-survival mode that rewards male dominance and female submission… It's one of the very few things that can. Sometims I wonder if it might not be the only thing. It enables us to imagine that alternative world. It gives us the vision and the tools to realize it in ourselves anywhere and everywhere that we are. In our music, in our writing, in our relationships, in our words. We must resist, resist, resist.

But I'm getting off track here. What is a straight woman?

All right. I'm going to read some theory here. So listen up. And while you listen, just let this question hang in the air out in front of you: "What is a straight woman?"

Okay… here goes. This is from Wikipedia:

> Some researchers assert *"that war and abductions (capture) were typical of human pre-history… When selection is intense and persistent, adaptive traits (such*

as capture–bonding) become universal to the population or species.

Partial activation of the capture–bonding psychological trait may lie behind battered-wife syndrome, military basic training, fraternity hazing, and sex practices such as sadism/masochism or bondage/discipline."

Professor Dee Graham has written a book that should be recommended reading for all fish desiring to know they are wet. It's call *Loving to Survive: Sexual Terror, Men's Violence, and Women's Lives*. That title has a double meaning. *Loving to Survive*: Talking about women who really, really want to survive, but also talking about what they have to do in order to survive: loving their enemy to survive.

Okay… Sister Dee Graham. She has come up with something very pertinent to this question of "What is a straight woman?" She has developed a theory around what she calls "Societal Stockholm Syndrome," or SSS.

In *Loving to Survive*, Sister Dee Graham argues that *all* women experience some degree of Stockholm Syndrome toward men because of their cultural conditioning. All women. All. No exceptions. All women. Some degree of Stockholm Syndrome. Can I get a witness?

How did she arrive at this theory? Well, she looked long and hard at Stockholm Syndrome, and she looked at the conditions necessary for the development of that syndrome. And there are four conditions that must be met... Now, I'm going to read these slowly, because this is sobering, sisters. This is a sobering question. Are we living in a world where all women have Societal Stockholm Syndrome, including us?

So here they are. All four conditions necessary for Stockholm Syndrome:

1. A perceived threat to survival and the belief that one's captor is willing to carry out that threat.

2. A perceived inability to escape.

3. A captive's perception of some small kindness from the captor within a context of terror.

4. Isolation from perspectives other than those of the captor.

Gonna read them again. Because our lives may depend on understanding this. Our real lives. Not our dissociated lives. But our real, authentic, chosen lives. Because, in the words of Sister Emily Bronte, "How can I live without my life?" And we know that billions of women are trying to do just that and then wondering why they feel so crazy.

1. A perceived threat to survival and the belief that one's captor is willing to carry out that threat.

2. A perceived inability to escape.

3. A captive's perception of some small kindness from the captor within a context of terror.

4. Isolation from perspectives other than those of the captor.

Sister Dee Graham asks if the four conditions conducive to Stockholm Syndrome exist at a societal level in male-female relations.

Well, sisters, do they?

Let's take a look.

1. *A perceived threat to survival and the belief that one's captor is willing to carry out that threat.*

Well, aside from the very recent history of women not being allowed to go to school, not being allowed to vote, not being allowed to own property, not being allowed to own our own children, not being allowed choices about pregnancy or child-rearing, not being allowed to own our wages, not being allowed to inherit, not being allowed to serve on juries, not being allowed to say they had been raped unless they were eighteen and a virgin... do we have reasons today to feel captive or threatened by men? And this is just our recent history here in the West. This year women in Saudi Arabia got the right to drive. It was 1971 before women won the right to vote in Switzerland. And we all know all kinds of rights are still denied to women all around the world.

So now let's look at this: Just a few years ago the Parents Television Council did a study. They reported 400 violent acts against women during prime time on three networks in just two months. 29 percent of the incidents were beatings, 18 percent credible threats of violence, 11 percent were shootings, 8 percent were rapes, 6 percent stabbings and 2 percent torture—and that in 92 percent of the incidents, graphic violence against women was *depicted*, not just implied. Furthermore 19% of the time, the women died as a result of the violence. That's just prime time.

Violence against women has risen 120% in five years, where violence against men and against both men and women only rose 2%.

And who's watching? Children. Girls. On average four hours of it a day. And we know from research that children watching violence become numb to the horror of violence, gradually accept violence as a way to solve problems, imitate the violence they observe on television and identify with certain characters, victims and/or victimizers. IDENTIFY WITH CERTAIN CHARACTERS. Identify with the perpetrator... in Freudian terms, this functions as an ego defense. In evolutionary terms, it serves the survival of the gene pool.

Another horrifying fact to consider in answer to this question of whether or not all women are perceiving threats to our survival. Prior to the age of four, a child does not have the synaptic capacity to distinguish between simulated violence on TV and actual violence. Yes, a child can be traumatized, and traumatized profoundly by graphic depictions of violence on television. Yes, a child can develop PTSD from images on a screen. Hence the numbness, identification with the perp, et cetera.

And then, of course, there are our histories. Every woman can name multiple female friends and family members who have survived—or not—acts of male violence, often from intimate partners. And, often... maybe even usually, she's got that history herself in her own personal life.

So I'm going to say yes to this first condition. Yes, all women on this planet perceive a threat to our survival from men and believe that men are perfectly capable of carrying out that threat. By the way, who is doing all that television programming, anyway? Do women really want to watch ourselves get tortured and murdered every night during prime time? Is Stockholm Syndrome some unfortunate by-product of this programming or is it the very *raison d'etre* for it... the reason why it exists in the first place.

Okay, Number Two: A perceived inability to escape. Oh, gosh. Let me count the ways... financially trapped in a marriage, unable to get enforcement of a restraining order, unable to get conviction of a rapist, children held as hostages, unable to get any kind of process at all in cases of military rape, inability to gain or keep employment if not practicing male-pleasing behaviors... ask any lesbian. And then of course, we know we are still raped and killed even when we dress so carefully, smile when we don't' feel like it, have a zillion locks on the doors, never go out at night, and so on and so on.

Yes, on two.

3. A captive's perception of some small kindness from the captor within a context of terror.

The one good man. The unbelievable courage and chivalry of a man who speaks on behalf of women. The exception that would disprove the rule.. Oh, gosh. They finally let us have the vote. Oh, gosh, we can have abortions... oh, wait... well maybe... but not in this state, not without parental permission... But they do let us have birth control... oh, but not some religions, and some pharmacists don't have to provide it... BUT... they do sometimes hold the door for us, and goddess help us if we fail to smile and thank them for it. Oh, yes... we do, we all do, we know we do fall all over ourselves for the small kindnesses of the exceptional man.

Three is a yes... yes, yes... oh, my, yes. Some men are so nice it makes it feel unfair to say anything bad about men at all... Oh, yes.

And four:

4. Isolation from perspectives other than those of the captor.

Sister Dee Graham, who wrote *Loving to Survive*, tells us there are two kinds of isolation: ideological isolation, and physical isolation. And both of these render us vulnerable to Stockholm Syndrome.

Ideological isolation… as in removing women and especially lesbians from history, all those father-son religions, one woman to every five men in films and TV. Scripts and screenplays overwhelmingly written by males, produced by males. Nothing but male-identified perspectives. Women's number-one-problem? How to get and keep a man. Please note, these cultural narratives do not focus on how to get away from men as a sex-caste, but on how to *get and keep* that one good exceptional man. The ideologically isolated woman interprets all her problems as individual and personal. She was in the wrong place at the wrong time, wearing the wrong thing. She does not see a social or political basis for the acts perpetrated against her. She experiences the extreme restrictions on her mobility as her own choice.

What about the physical isolation? Isn't the officially sanctioned model a woman living off with a man and with her children somewhere? Aren't women nervous when they do anything that doesn't involve men? Aren't women always so eager to insist that they are not lesbians or men-haters? Too much hanging out with other women will cost her male approval, protection and privilege. Absolutely. ABSOLUTELY.

So… isolated? Yes.

Do the four conditions exist SOCIETALLY so that *all* women experience some degree of Stockholm Syndrome toward men because of our cultural conditioning?

Yes.

And what do we do about it? Some women identify with their Societal Stockholm Syndome wholeheartedly, empathizing, sympathizing, justifying, rationalizing, apologizing for, and defending men... Some negotiate their SSS, focusing like the Marines on finding a few good men. And some fight it. Some work like hell to create alternative communities of women where we do have the resources for survival and are not dependent on male approval. Some women fight our amygdalas, our primitive brains. Some women model astoundingly courageous and creative responses other than capitulation and trauma bonding.

These women who are resisting the culture of Societal Stockholm Syndrome, who pay such a price in terms of isolation, are the lesbian-feminists... the Sisterhood of the Sacred Synapse. And when they ask us, "What is a lesbian?" let us turn that question on its head by an informed inquiry into the nature of the straight woman, the woman who sleeps with the enemy.

Blessed be.

Sermon on Betrayal

Sisters, let's talk about betrayal. Because as women, we have all been betrayed, and as lesbians, we have all been betrayed.

First off, what is betrayal? Well... here's what the dictionary has to say about it:

> *"To give aid or information to an enemy, or to deliver into the hands of an enemy in violation of trust or allegiance."*

Well, now this is very interesting, if you substitute the word "perpetrator" for "enemy." Today, talking about betrayal, we're going to be calling on one of the saints of the Lesbian Tent Revival, Saint Judith Herman, who wrote the first book on Complex PTSD, describing the psychological effects of child abuse, and how to recover from it. The book is *Trauma and Recovery*, and it is a book that has allowed millions to realize we are not crazy, just victimized and violated, and that there are very real wounds from that, and that we can recover from them.

Okay... so Saint Judith said, "It is very tempting to take the side of the perpetrator. All the perpetrator asks is that the bystander do nothing. He appeals to the universal desire to see, hear, and speak no evil. The victim, on the contrary, asks the bystander to share the burden of pain. The victim demands action, engagement, and remembering."

So if you synapse this up with the definition of betrayal about aiding or delivering up to an enemy, you get a linkage that tells a great truth about our culture: It's very easy to betray. In fact, it's going to take an effort *not* to betray.

And why is that? Because we live in a culture that is owned by the hoarders, and they represent the interests of a very, very small minority of folks: white, heterosexual, male, or those who identify with those values and interests. It's a culture designed to exploit or destroy the rest of us. If we are not challenging these values and this culture and these institutions, then we are going to be aiding the enemy and delivering ourselves and each other over to the enemy. We are going to be betrayed and betraying.

Another definition of "betray" is "to be false or disloyal to." Which means we have to figure out what it is we are being loyal to. And in this culture, this causes a lot of confusion. Are we loyal to our families? And if we are, does loyalty mean keeping the family secrets, because telling them might make the family vulnerable? And does this go for lesbians, too? Our lesbian families of choice and communities harbor secrets, too. What about loyalty to our church? What does that mean, if our church has judgments about sexual orientation and we are lesbian? And this isn't just about lesbian Baptists or Catholics… What about 12-step programs that encourage us to mind our own business? How does that fit with speaking out or intervening when injustice to others is occuring? Or what about ideologies of passivism? How do we respond to militant responses to aggression? Are we loyal to our country? And

134

what does that mean when we disagree with national policies? And how about loyalty to a political party... how much should we be willing to overlook in the name of solidarity?

Seems like any time we take any kind of stand for our own truth, we're going to be betraying somebody or something, and sometimes that can be something or somebody inside ourselves. If you want to be careful not to betray anyone anytime, you might choose to never speak up at all... but, as Judith Herman has pointed out, this is going to result in the most massive betrayals of all.

So... sisters. No easy answers. Our best defense against betraying people or things we hold dear is to synapse early and often—to do our very best thinking, use our most conscientious process, and be ready to step up with accountability when we do end up betraying.

Okay, but what about when we are betrayed? Here is Saint Judith again: "The conflict between the will to deny horrible events and the will to proclaim them aloud is the central dialectic of psychological trauma."

"The central dialectic of psychological trauma." In other words, that's what makes trauma, trauma. Accepting what cannot be accepted. Telling what cannot be told. The mind just bounces back and forth between strategies for surviving: "This can't be happening/this really is happening." "I have to deny this to survive/ I have to accept this to survive." Trauma affects us the way it does, precisely because of this central conflict. It can stay frozen or repressed. It can remain unassimilated. It can leak out into all our interactions. It can warp all our perceptions and give us a distorted sense of reality and who we are.

When we are betrayed, and I mean seriously betrayed, we are traumatized. "I have to trust this person or this institution/ I have to understand that this person or this institution can't be trusted." Accepting the unacceptable. I mean, sisters, really think about that sentence. "Accept. The. Unacceptable." If your brain is working well, you won't be able to assimilate that sentence. The two concepts are completely incompatible.

To assimilate trauma, we have to learn to dismantle the "unacceptable" part. Often the "unacceptable" is based on the fact that we are dependent. As children we cannot accept that our parents are dangerous, because it appears more dangerous to be without parents. As employees, we may feel that we cannot afford to know that our employer is abusing us or violating ethics, because we feel that we need the job. As students, we might feel that we cannot accept that our teacher is a sexual predator, because we feel we need the passing grade. Many lesbians have experienced their lesbianism as traumatic, because they could not accept the potential loss of family or spiritual community.

Denial is taking the wrong end of the stick. Denial is dismantling the need to accept the betrayal by saying or pretending it never happened… explaining it away, forgetting about it, and so on. Often this can seem like the easiest thing to do—except for that PTSD thing. Unassimilated trauma can affect every single aspect of your life, and maybe you aren't

136

even realizing it, but it can and it does. Believe it or not, it's easier and more cost efficient to work with the second part of the equation: Work on the "unacceptable." Work to find a way to accept the betrayal. This can and often does mean seeking out alternative support systems or institutions.

And while we are talking about the work-arounds, here's something worth considering: researchers are beginning to suspect that massive, pervasive, betrayal trauma in childhood can actually change some of the chemistry in the brain. We already know that regular trauma can do that. That's what all that fight-flight-freeze business is about… heightened responses in the brain.

Okay… what's the neurophysiology, the brain chemistry of relationships? Well, one of the key factors appears to be oxytocin. Oxytocin has been called "the bonding hormone." It has been associated with orgasm, social recognition, pair bonding, anxiety, and maternal behaviors. The "bonding hormone." Obviously, we evolved into producing this, because bonding helped us survive as a species. Orgasm would lead us to seek partners for sex, and then oxytocin would help us out with the pair bonding and maternal so-called instincts that would help the female and her offspring survive pregnancy and gestation. The humans with the highest oxytocin production might survive better, so natural selection would favor those oxytocin producers.

But what if all this bonding didn't help you survive? What if your parents were addicts or sexual predators or violent? In that case, the oxytocin would just keep you coming back for more. In the face of betrayal trauma from family of birth, it might be adaptive for a child to develop some mechanism for shutting down oxytocin. And, guess what? That appears to be exactly what is happening. They call it "oxytocin dysregulation," and it appears to be linked to betrayal trauma. Which makes sense. Psychologists have noted for a long time that badly hurt children often have difficulty with trust. They use terms like "failure to bond" or "attachment disorder."

Sisters, "failure" and "disorder" are unfair words to apply to someone who is trying desperately to succeed in survival and bring order to a chaotic universe. We have to synapse deeply around a boatload of the terminology applied to trauma survivors, because this terminology can be seriously victim-blaming, and those of us who survived don't need any more of that. In fact, as most of us know, the whole field of psychiatry and psychology has been rife with betrayals of women and children and survivors of trauma.

So, sisters, what if we have developed this shutdown of oxytocin production or reception? What if we have this "oxytocin dysregulation" going on? Well... now we are in a frontier. I don't think anybody really knows if we can turn it back on again. Maybe we can and maybe we can't. But what I do know is this: People who have learned not to trust can learn to trust. It takes work, but we can do it. We can learn that the whole world is not full of evil, damaged people. We can learn that there are safe people, and we can learn the difference between acceptable expressions of human weakness and unacceptable levels. We can learn to confront behavior and ask for accountability and we can learn to detach. We learn that we can be uncomfortable and still not be endangered. Most of all, we can learn the benefits of belonging to a community, of bonding with an institution. We can learn the ways that family and partners enhance our lives, in spite of the ways that they can and will compromise us.

What makes this difficult is that those of us who lack the psychic or biochemical component for bonding often are very clear about the costs of bonding, but we don't see the benefits. We are quick to cut and run and tell ourselves that we really dodged a bullet on that one. We test people until they fail and then we isolate. In the words of Judith Herman, "Over time as most people fail the survivor's exacting test of trustworthiness, she tends to withdraw from relationships. The isolation of the survivor thus persists even after she is free."

If we were badly betrayed as children, we are not especially incentivized to learn the benefits of closeness. This is where we might have to engage the intellect. This is where we might have to have an intellectual understanding of betrayal trauma and its impact. This is where we might have to come to an intellectual understanding that our best thinking is very possibly quite distorted and that we are missing out on something wonderful and something productive, because of left-over, over-protective behaviors.

So, sisters, what about "stable relationships over time?" What do they take? Consistency and accountability. Showing up on a regular basis. You can build a stable, meaningful relationship by touching base with someone in a weekly or monthly phone call, monthly coffee… You don't have to live with them. You don't have to marry them. You don't have to agree on everything. You don't have to vote the same way, believe the same way. You have to just show up regularly, be reliable, be accountable. It's not really a big deal. It's a one-day-at-a-time thing. And notice, I did not say, "You have to care." Obviously, you have to care, but it's *how you show that care* that will determine whether or not you develop a stable and healthy relationship."

If it doesn't come naturally, you can engage the intellect. That's the beauty of understanding trauma. We're not stuck with the way our brain works. We can stand back and look at it and make different choices.

One of the reasons why 12-Step programs work is that they use a format that makes it impossible to express judgment or criticism. These are two things that impair ability to trust. These are safe places to explore getting know the truth of other peoples' lives and getting to test the waters about sharing our own truths.

Sisters, trauma is some real shit. And betrayal trauma is a big deal. Just because the wounds are invisible, doesn't mean they are any less severe than what happens to you in a car accident. The problem is that, with many betrayal traumas, nobody calls 911, no ambulance comes. You lie on the metaphorical side of the road, hemorrhaging trust, and eventually you get up and, since there is often no witness to name or validate what happened, you learn to pretend it didn't... but you don't go near roads or vehicles. You spend your life on foot, avoiding traffic of any kind. As we say in Maine, "That's livin' small."

Folksinger Walt Cronin has a line "Healing comes from looking closely." Sisters, look closely. Have the courage to look closely at what happened to you and the courage to look closely at what is happening to other people.

Sometimes it's easier to talk about how our families have betrayed us than to talk about—really talk about—how institutions have betrayed us. But they are connected. Unrecovered survivors of betrayal trauma grow up to be vulnerable to other betrayals, and also to become betrayers ourselves. The kind of mental compartmentalization that enables victims to deny the original betrayal is like a filing system. It's where they can store memories of other betrayals, including those they perpetrate: "I didn't really mean that." "I wasn't all that serious." "I didn't really hurt anyone… and besides I was justified." Sisters, it's all about the synapse. Be careful what you wall off. It can become a repository for all kinds of things.

When we are personally betrayed by family or friends, there are institutions that do become involved. There are religious institutions, government institutions, educational institutions that often have a mandate to step in, to advocate for the victim. What if they don't? What if they side with the perpetrator instead? And, remember what Judith Herman said:

> *"It is very tempting to take the side of the perpetrator. All the perpetrator asks is that the bystander do nothing. He appeals to the universal desire to see, hear, and speak no evil. The victim, on the contrary, asks the*

bystander to share the burden of pain. The victim demands action, engagement, and remembering."

You know, Sister Carolyn believes in repeating herself. The patriarchy repeats itself all the time, all day long. We see about 5000 commercial messages a day. Don't be afraid to repeat yourself. It's called laying synaptic tracks. Intentional ones. Talk to yourself, sisters. Talk to yourself. A lot.

So, again:

"It is very tempting to take the side of the perpetrator. All the perpetrator asks is that the bystander do nothing. He appeals to the universal desire to see, hear, and speak no evil. The victim, on the contrary, asks the bystander to share the burden of pain. The victim demands action, engagement, and remembering."

All these institutions have to do is nothing. The teacher who ignores the bruises. The Catholic administrator who sends the charge of child sexual abuse up the line without follow-up. The military officer who decides not to investigate the story of the rape. The family who continues to invite the perpetrator to Thanksgiving dinner, and tells you it's your choice to attend.

The betrayal by the institution can be even more damaging than the original trauma. We know that the severity of PTSD is more a function of how long it takes for a community to respond appropriately than it is a function of the severity of the original incident. The rapist may be a crazed individual, but what happens to us when we realize that our entire community or family of birth takes their side? What's their excuse?

Betrayal by institutions is a big deal, sisters, and we live in a world where nearly all of them are designed to betray us. This is something we have to know. And to know this is truly "accepting the unacceptable." We have to find institutions that will not betray us, and if we can't, then we need to create them. These may disappoint us. But they will not deliver us to the enemy. We have to take responsibility for finding and building our own.

I have a theory about this betrayal business. I believe that the betrayals are coming so thick and fast now, especially the institutional ones, that the whole point is to produce a population incapable of authentic bonding, whose idea of friendship is strangers on Facebook, whose idea of intimacy is sex, and whose sense of belonging stems from dependence on identifying with the corporate interests that are destroying the planet.

We have to work, sisters, work, on resisting this. We have to look closely. *Look closely*. I mean it Look closely. And it's going to cost you. Judith Herman knew this. I'm going to give her the last word here. She is talking about the attacks on therapists who are doing work with trauma survivors, but it's bigger than that. It's all of us who are attempting to know what we know, to be authentic, to stay connected with all forms of life on this planet.

Here's Judith Herman:

"The dialectic of trauma is playing itself out once again. It is worth remembering that this is not the first time in history that those who have listened closely to trauma survivors have been subject to challenge. Nor will it be the last. In the past few years, many clinicians have had to learn to deal with the same tactics of harassment and intimidation that grassroots advocates for women, children and other oppressed groups have long endured. We, the bystanders, have had to look within ourselves to find some small portion of the courage that victims of violence must muster every day.

Some attacks have been downright silly; many have been quite ugly. Though frightening, these attacks are an implicit tribute to the power of the healing relationship. They remind us that creating a protected space where survivors can speak their truth is an act of liberation. They remind us that bearing witness, even within the confines of that sanctuary, is an act of solidarity. They remind us also that moral neutrality in the conflict between victim and perpetrator is not an option. Like all other bystanders, therapists are sometimes forced to take sides. Those who stand with the victim will inevitably have to face the perpetrator's unmasked fury. For many of us, there can be no greater honor."

Blessed be!

Sermon on Secrets of Salience

Sisters, I want to talk about saliency. Which is the quality of being salient. Gotta love it when the dictionary does that.

So what does "salient" mean?

First and foremost, it means "most noticeable or important."

We are the Sisterhood of the Sacred Synapse. And that is because we take our ability to think seriously. Because we understand thinking radically to be a privilege, a prerogative, and an obligation. Thinking deeply, freely, and with optimal synapsing going on. Because we know that we have charge of our thinking, and that it is a sacred charge. Yes, it is. So how does the brain pick out what to notice? How does it decide what is important?

Okay. Let's imagine that you are cruising down the strip in Las Vegas. And there are a zillion neon lights all competing for your attention. And they have lights blinking on and off, and going around in a circle and then reversing direction. All different colors. And they are advertising nearly naked women, and they are advertising free drinks in the casino, and they are advertising gambling. It's a regular candy store for addictions and compulsions. And yet, with all this extravagant competition for our attention, what is it that our brain will notice? Probably the humblest light display on the boulevard. A little rectangular box with a red, green and yellow light.

That's right. The traffic light. It's not neon. It isn't spelling out any words. It doesn't speak to any addictions. It's not winking or blinking or going in circles. Why does our brain give it our full attention? Because the brain knows that if we ignore it, we could die. It has the most salient information on the whole strip. We ignore the traffic light at our peril. Because if we die, there won't be any nearly naked women, any booze, any gambling. It's over. We're dead. It trumps everything else. And most of us will focus on that light without even making an effort. Our brain has been programmed to give the traffic light priority.

Our brain has salience filters. They can keep us alive, like the example of the traffic light in Las Vegas. But sometimes we can have salience filters that do not serve us very well. Those filters may have been put into place without our knowledge or choosing.

Because we are animals. Now, you know we harp on that in the Lesbian Tent Revival. We do. We are primates, mammals, animals. We are hard-wired for perpetuation of the gene pool. Not survival of the fittest, but perpetuation of the gene pool. That's important for us, as females, to remember. We are wired to breed early and often, and to do whatever bonding we have to in order to ensure the survival of our offspring. If you do not see this as your main goal in life, then you might want to check how your salience filters might be setting you up for compulsive romance with inappropriate partners... and so on. But I have a ton of sermons on that subject, so we won't dwell on that.

146

But here's another layer of subconscious salience filtering: Childhood. And especially childhood trauma. If we grew up in dangerous environments, our brains may have learned to filter everything for signs—even little signs—of danger. Good thing to do in a war zone. Acts of kindness, signals of common interests are more like distractions when you are in a situation where a wrong move might cost you your life or bring on an act of violence. You might have a brain that filters out good stuff like a sieve with holes that are too large. You might have a brain that filters almost everything out... including what might make life easier or more enjoyable. If someone so much as disagrees with you... boom, out they go. Possible source of conflict! Warning! Warning! Danger!

Some of us have salience filters that were set for another time, another planet. Planet Childhood. We need to check that we don't carry those filters into adulthood, where we have agency and options and where we don't have to live in a traumatized state.

Sisters, our salience filters—the way we choose what to notice, the way we choose what is important—can destroy our lives. They can also wreck our quality of experience. If we are focused on avoiding danger all the time, we will miss so, so, so many opportunities for joy and creativity. Sisters, many of us have salience filters that are designed to filter out anything with any degree of risk. I understand that. Sisters, I do. PTSD and Complex PTSD will do that. No such thing as "moderate risk" when one is talking about being triggered all the time. The salience filters when we are in a post-traumatic state should be temporarily set on high alert, but that post-traumatic state should be temporary also. So let's get the healing we need so that we can tolerate the moderate risk that is necessary for deeply meaningful lives.

So how do we get control of our salience filters? How do we program or reprogram the brain for what to notice, for what is most important? Synapse, sisters. The sacrament that is at the heart of the Lesbian Tent Revival. We connect neurons, we spark the gap. Sisters, we THINK. Deeply, radically, freely. We *think*. Neurons that fire together, wire together. That's how we form the web of our thinking. And that web is also a filter, a sieve.

We synapse in order to learn about ourselves. What are we noticing as we cruise down the strip of life? Are we noticing what we would *choose* to notice, or are we sitting back on the sofas of life clicking through the remote… and sisters, it *is* the remote, and then pretending that selecting a patriarchal program is some form of choice? Or are we CHOOSING what is important, and then going out with our pith helmet and our magnifying glass and actively looking for it in difficult but breathtaking places?

Are we fully aware of the price we pay for our salience settings? Are we really aware of the cost of those high settings for danger? Do we really *get* how intolerance of risk robs us of joy? How buying into consumerism numbs us to the satisfactions of living a customized life? Are we aware of the price we pay for active addiction and compulsive behaviors?

Sisters, *carpe salience*! Seize your salience filters! Take control of your thinking! Be in charge of what gets your attention!

And nowhere is that more important than at this last Michigan Festival. Sisters, let's not miss it. Let's not go through it with blinders on, focused on shit that scared us as children or that will perpetuate the species. For crying out loud! Let us decide what we want to give our attention to, because we will never have another opportunity. Sisters, this is it. Let us not miss our own Festival, our own life, because we are focused on shit that makes us miserable and traps us in some story of perpetual danger, perpetual inferiority, perpetual fear.

So hold that thought, sisters. We're going to digress. We're going to talk about mental illness, because you know we do a lot of that here. We talk a lot about mental illness, because that can be a highly political issue in a patriarchal world that rewards us so heavily for violating our own truths.

So here we go... We are going to talk about schizophrenia today. Here's Wikipedia's layman definition: "a mental disorder often characterized by abnormal social behavior and failure to recognize what is real." Failure to recognize what is real. Yeah, hold onto that one. Okay, Wikipedia again: "Common symptoms include false beliefs, unclear or confused thinking, auditory hallucinations, reduced social engagement and emotional expression, and inactivity." Hold onto that, too. And finally: "Diagnosis is based on observed behavior and the person's reported experiences."

Schizophrenia. Now... there have been some new studies about schizophrenia that are sending therapists in new directions. There have been studies that are indicating that schizophrenia may have something to do with salience... that folks suffering from schizophrenia may have some kind of failed salience filters—eccentric ideas about what is and what is not salient, eccentric ideas about what to notice, about what is important. They are beginning to suspect that the person with schizophrenia might be having difficulty filtering, might be attempting to make a coherent story or to extract meaning from an overwhelming amount of stimuli, without the usual consensus-based idea of what is salient. Like driving down that strip in Las Vegas and focusing on the wrong lights at the intersection.

Sisters, we all need food, shelter, and water. But we also need coherence. We need to be able to make sense of what we are experiencing, to make sense of our lives. To this end we tell ourselves stories: "She just looked at me like that, because she hates me. And she hates me because..." "This is happening to me, because I dot-dot-dot." We make observations, we collect data, and then we try to make sense of it.

And I do love to act like I can quote Russian writers, because it makes me look smart. So I'm going to quote Dostoevsky. He said:

> *"No one can live without being able to explain to themselves what is happening to them, and if one day they should no longer be able to explain anything to*

themselves, they would say they had gone mad, and this would be for them the last explanation."

What does that have to do with salience? Well, the brain picks out what we focus on, and then we have to make that make sense to ourselves. In a perfect world, the brain is choosing to focus on things that will help us lead joyous and productive lives... but what if our salience filters are out of whack? What if we are collecting data that is really strange and irrelevant, but then, because our brains have picked it out, we have to hammer out a story with it?

Sisters, folks who suffer from schizophrenia can see a billboard and believe that it is communicating a secret message for them, a message of warning or harassment that is only meant for them... from an enemy or a higher power, or a dead person. Is that "crazy," or could it be that their brain is picking random things—like a billboard on the side of the road— to focus on, and then trying to figure out exactly why this is so urgent to focus on. Putting the cart before the horse. Tail wagging the dog.

So, sisters, let's do an exercise right now on salience. I am going to ask you all to close your eyes and then open them, and then imagine that the very first thing you happen to see will be the most salient object in this moment, in this environment. And then I invite each of you to explain to yourself, to make up a story, about why that particular thing you are focused on is so urgently important right now. Sisters, if you open your eyes, and a blade of grass is the first thing you see, then that blade of grass is the most significant thing in your life. You must understand its meaning, what it is trying to say to you that makes it so important. It is saving your life or else putting your life in danger... OBVIOUSLY, because your brain is giving it that level of priority. So your job is to figure out how or why? All right... so let's do this exercise. It's an exercise in storytelling, which we are doing to ourselves all the time... only we usually are not hyperfocused on random and irrelevant things. So, for this exercise, no explanation is too bizarre, too paranoid, too paranormal. Go where you have to go to make sense of what your brain has selected. But the one thing that you cannot do in this exercise is question the salience of the object.

So... let's all take a minute to do this. Really stop reading or stop the podcast. Take a few minutes right now. Close your eyes. Open them. First thing you see is the most salient thing in your life right now. And now, you have to figure out why.

Okay. So what did you come up with? I'm going to guess that you came up with a narrative that involved some of those definitions of schizophrenia... like "false beliefs, unclear or confused thinking, and auditory hallucinations." If the object was warning or threatening you, you might have ended up with a story that would qualify for "paranoid schizophrenia."

And I'll bet if you went through your day holding onto this exercise and allowing it to shape your other interactions and experiences, you might end up with another part of that definition of schizophrenia, namely "reduced social engagement and emotional expression, and inactivity."

Why are we spending so much time on schizophrenia? Because I want to bring home how critical your salience filter can be to your mental health. Because I want you to understand just how much your salience filter settings can ruin or warp your experience of this last Festival... or how much they can enhance and elevate it. And the choice is yours. Sisters, barring a meteor falling on Hart, we will all pretty much have the Festival that our salience filters allow us to have. That's the truth. And the truth is we have control over those filters. It might take some effort, but we can become aware of how we filter our experiences, and how we change that.

What we give our attention to, grows. That's the truth. Or as George Lucas put it, "Always remember, your focus determines your reality." We should all notice what is important, but that can go the other way, too... like in our little experiment. What we notice frequently, or attentively, will become important... even if it shouldn't. And that can make us honestly and truly, clinically crazy.

Salience can be manipulated, imposed, legislated. During the Chinese Cultural Revolution, for example, one could be sent to a prison camp for possessing a recording of a Beethoven symphony. Suddenly the presence of what had formerly been an everyday object in a home became one of the most salient facts about that home. Legislated salience.

Our biology, our childhoods, and our culture are always trying to program our salience filters. They are always trying to tell us what we should notice, what should be important to us. We

153

MUST seize control of our salience. We must synapse, sisters. And we must synapse specifically to CHOOSE what we want to experience and take away from this most precious Michigan Womyn's Music Festival. If we go through it with our usual filters, we will have our usual experience. And it may be an experience of sexual predation, sisters... because we can be that way if we are in the throes of sexual compulsion. It may be an experience of everyone else being members of a club we can't join, if that's the story of our childhood. It may be an experience of physical discomfort over camping and long lines, because we have learned to hyperfocus on negative sensations.

Or it may be an experience of amazement and wonder, of breathtaking levels of trust with strangers, of radically broadened possibilities from contact with other cultures.

It's up to us. Or, rather, to our salience filters. Let us choose right now two or three things that we want to be most salient about this festival. Joy? Beauty? Nature? Sisterhood? Creativity? Adventure? Let us pick our priorities and then let us be conscious about noticing what we notice. It's a choice!

Sisters, we have all come this long, long way to get here... and I am speaking metaphysically as much as geographically. Let us not miss our own Festival.

Seize the salience!

Blessed be!

Sermon on Radical Humility

"That word you keep using... I do not think it means what you think it means."—Inigo Montoya from *The Princess Bride*

So what is that word that I do not think means what you think it means? Reality. Sister Carolyn here, from the Sisterhood of the Sacred Synapse. Welcome to the Lesbian Tent Revival Radio Hour podcast. Sisters, this is a very special podcast, because it is the last sermon from the last Tent Revival at the last Michigan Womyn's Music Festival.

And BECAUSE of that, sisters, we are going to doing our most epically radical thinking of all time, ever... because that is going to help us with our grief. Yes, it will sisters. It will move us forward, together.

All right... so here we go...

Today, sisters, is going to be the culmination of nine years of the Lesbian Tent Revival. That's five sermons every year for a grand total of forty-five. Today is when we are going to fire up those synapses and ride them all the way to the end of the line. Today Sister Carolyn is going to initiate you into the most secret and most sacred mantra of the Sisterhood of the Sacred Synapse. And with that Secret will come great power and great responsibility.... Sisters, are you ready? Because, after today you will never see anything the same way again. Are you ready? Because after today everything you thought was true is going to change. Are you ready, sisters, in the words of Robin Morgan, "to go sane?"

All right.

Now, we're about to go deep here… So just remember, this is about the end of Festival. We are needing to go deep.

So…

The secret of the Sisterhood of the Sacred Synapse is summed up in the immortal words of Inigo Montoya of that legendary film *The Princess Bride*. And here it is: *"That word you keep using… I do not think it means what you think it means."*

Can you say that with me? This, my sisters, is a sacred incantation that can restore sanity in even the direst circumstances. Or, barring that, at least make you feel foolish… which is the next best thing.

Don't take my word for it. Don't even take *The Princess Bride*'s word for it. This is what the renowned physicist Neils Bohr had to say about it: "Everything we call real is made of things that cannot be regarded as real." "Everything." As in "every thing." Everything. Neils Bohr does not think that word means what you think it means. And by the way, when he was born, his mother took one look at him and said, "Bit of a Bohr, isn't he?"

Just checking… Now, stay with me, sisters. This is about the end of the Festival. I promise.

In my generation the famous double helix of DNA had just been discovered, and scientists—and they were 99% men in that era—were utterly enamored with the whole building-blocks thing. According to them, we all learned in school that the atom was the basic Lego of the Legoland of matter, or what we call "reality." And we all had these Styrofoam balls with little sticks, and we would build models of this atom, with the protons and neutrons in the middle and the electrons sticking out around it. And we made molecules out the atoms, and we all knew that atoms and molecules were the building blocks of matter. The secrets of the universe had been boiled down to the ultimate Lego.

But of course, this was just a fantasy, because the real secret of the universe is contained in... what? Those words of Inigo Montoya. Which are...?

"That word you keep using... I do not think it means what you think it means."

Sooner or later, somebody would get the idea of trying to take apart the ultimate Lego, and eventually they did. And they did not find mini-Legos, or sub-Legos. What they found was that the Lego was not really there at all. Not the way we thought it was. Not solid. Not a thing. That found something that acted like a wave sometimes—like energy, but then, sometimes it acted like a particle—like matter. If you could locate it in space, it didn't exist in time. If you could locate it in time, it was not present in space. So what the hell was it? If the universe was not made up of atomic Legos, then what was it made up of? Sisters, the answer is something we at Michigan have known in our hearts all along. It is made up of probabilities. That's the nearest best definition.

That's us. That's this Land. That's everything. Every thing. Probability. We are experiencing what appears likely. We know something about this, because we know that what is likely on the Land is highly unlikely out in Area 51 (our term for the other fifty-one weeks of the year lived off the Land. This is a joking reference to the notorious "Area 51" that was a highly classified area of the Nevada nuclear test range.) We also know that most of what is likely in Area 51 is unlikely at Fest. We dykes have changed the odds. We experience a different probability here.

But we have to keep going, sisters. Get back on the synaptic bus... Like I said, we are going to the end of the line today. All the way to the end.

Okay. So the Lego is not the Lego. And that means Legoland isn't really Legoland. Hold that thought.

So now we're going to Flatland. How many of you have read that book, *Flatland*?

Okay, Flatland is a two-dimensional world like a piece of paper. Only paper isn't really two-dimensional, because it has depth... Tiny depth, but depth. And a two-dimensional world ONLY has length and width. Yes, it only exists in the mind.

So that's Flatland. And there are two-dimensional people who live on it. So let's imagine that someone pokes a line through their flat plane, like sticking a needle through a piece of paper—only paper that has no thickness, just width and length—two dimensions. What are these inhabitants of that plane going to experience? They can't see anything in the third dimension. All they will see is that a dot has appeared on their landscape. They can't see the needle, because it is above and below Flatland. They have no concept, no language for a needle being poked through their plane. A dot appears. They are attempting to explain a phenomenon from the third dimension in the language of only two dimensions. And that means they have a limited, incomplete, and distorted perception of what they are experiencing. I'm going to say that again: The Flatlanders have a limited, incomplete, and distorted perception of what they are experiencing, because they have no understanding of a third dimension.

Now… what if a ping pong ball from outer space gets stuck in the middle of Flatland. They can't experience a sphere. They can't conceive of a ping pong ball… or any kind of ball, because a ball has three dimensions. They will see where something is cutting through or discoloring the surface of Flatland, but they can't see above or below the plane they are on.

So, some of you are thinking, "Well… they see a circle." But, stay with me here. No, they don't see a circle. If you are in a lake, a very flat lake with no waves, and your eyes are on a level with the surface of the water, and there is a hula hoop floating in front of you… you don't see it as a hoop. You just see it as a line. Your eyes are on the same plane as the hoop. Are you still with me?

That's what the Flatlanders see: a line. They don't see a circle. They see a line. So let's say they decide to explore it. They walk toward it. They want to walk to the end of it, to measure it… but sisters, it's a circle, so what is going to happen? As they walk along this "line," they will find that it just keeps extending. They don't know they are traveling in a circle. They just know that the line is never-ending. AND, listen up… here is what they might say to themselves to explain it: "Every time I take a step, the line gets that much longer. It is growing and moving in time."

But we can see the pingpong ball. Nothing is growing or moving. The Flatlanders are again getting it wrong, because they are trying to describe a three-dimensional phenomenon in terms of two dimensions. Their perception of TIME is just a mistaken way to explain what they lack words to explain.

Sisters. We live in three dimensions. There may well be four dimensions. Or five. Or a thousand. We only perceive three. We try to explain everything to ourselves in terms of length, width, breadth. And then we say "time." But time could just be like the Flatlanders' time. Time could just be our mistaken way of describing phenomena from these other dimensions outside our understanding.

"Time." *"That word you keep using… I do not think it means what you think it means."*

"Reality." *"That word you keep using... I do not think it means what you think it means."*

So. No Legos. No Legoland. Limited, three dimensional explanations for everything from all other possible dimensions.

This IS about the Festival, so stay with me, sisters. Ride this train all the way to the end!

We are beginning to get a picture here of how very little we know and how little we understand, and how what we think we understand may be completely wrong. Neils Bohr certainly told us that flat out: "Everything we call real is made of things that cannot be regarded as real." Sisters, we are approaching an enormous force field called Radical Humility.

Not to be confused with humility-humility. Regular old humility can be a terrible thing for women. Regular humility can be like "Dorothy the Meek and Lowly" facing the great Wizard of Oz. It can be part of how patriarchy conditions women to be subordinate, compliant, and so on.

Radical Humility is something very powerful, because it is about going to the very *roots of self-awareness.* Radical Humility is the beginning of wisdom. It is using all our synapses to understand that what we know is only a sliver of a fraction of what there is to know. Radical Humility opens us up to vast biophilic—that's "life-loving"— connections with all forms of life as we know them. It opens us up to other dimensions of knowing. It CREATES SPACE for possibility.

And where we create space for possibility, we can create collective space for probability… and as we have just learned, probability is actually the underlying principle of what we call reality. Probability is the real Lego of what we experience as reality. I want to repeat this sentence, because it's so important: "Where we create space for possibility, we can create collective space for probability."

So, sisters, we must embrace our limitations. We must embrace our ignorance. We must move into Radical Humility like a cottage that is custom built for our needs—no more, no less. Radical Humility, my sisters. Make friends with it. Because we don't know shit. Seriously.

Okay. So we talked about Flatland, and how screwed up it is to try to interpret things that are outside our limited dimensions. And, sisters, we have absolutely no grounds to assume that, just because we only experience three dimensions, that's all there is.

So… Hold onto that.

Now, we're going to talk about the Cat and the Slat. And, yes, this has everything to do with the end of the Michigan Festival, so stay with me. We are going the long way home here.

Okay. Let's say we are looking at a fence. And it's very tall and very wide, so we can't see over it or around it. But it has one of the slats knocked out, so there is about a four-inch slit where we can see some of what's going on on the other side.

Now, let's say a cat walks by. Let's say left to right. Let's say we have never seen a cat before and we don't know what it is. So all we know is what we see through the slat. We see a round whiskery thing, and then a kind of bigger oval thing, and then a long pointy thing. We don't know what we're seeing. But let's say there is a lesbian on the other side with a ton of cats and she's feeding them. So there are a number of cats crossing left to right and we are seeing all this through the slat.

Remember, we don't really know what a cat is, because we can't see it all at once. We only see parts and they always come in a certain sequence at a fairly consistent speed. We may decide that what we are seeing is an event. It is an event that lasts about three or four seconds (depending on how fast the cat is moving). Maybe we call it the "Fuzz Event." It begins with the "Round Whiskery Event," which will always cause the "Oval Event" to happen immediately after, which will then cause the "Long Pointy Event." Those are the three stages of the overall "Fuzz Event." Every time we see the Round Whiskery Event, we can count on the Oval and then the Long Pointy Events." And then it's over.

But let's say one of the cats stops to lick her genitals, because you know how they do... Wait! Suddenly the Round Whiskery event stops. It's not immediately followed by the Oval Event. Time has stopped. Something miraculous or terrifying is happening. There has been a disruption in the normal sequence of the Fuzz Event. We are greatly relieved when the Long Pointy Event finally occurs.

Just like the folks in Flatland, we are not really getting the full picture. We are not understanding that what we are experiencing is not an event, but an entity: a whole cat. The head does not cause the tail. They are not events separated in time. They exist simultaneously. But we experience them separated in time because we are having to experience the cat through a narrow slat. The cat knows nothing of our ignorance and is blissfully existing all at once on the other side of the wall.

Sisters. Work with me here. There is this event. I say EVENT. The Michigan Festival. It has a Wait-in-Line Event, then an Opening Gate Event, then an Opening Night Event, then a Nutloaf Event, and then a Sunday Night Event. And then the Festival is over. It didn't go somewhere. It just is over, gone, disappeared.

Well, sisters. We are experiencing this Festival through our eye slits, which aren't even as big as the slat in the fence. We are experiencing it through tiny little ear holes. We are just possibly making the same mistake as our mythical Slat-watchers are. Maybe the Michigan Festival on the other side of our narrow perceptional fence is still going on, just like the cat. Maybe, like the cat, those things we call events separated in time are not separate at all, but simultaneously existing... That Nutloaf Night and the Opening Gate are both happening at the same time, part of an ENTITY, not an event at all.

Furthermore... what if that first Festival and then the second Festival, and then the third, and the fifteenth, and the twenty-eighth... what if those are part of an entity... not separate events at all, not over, not separated in time. What if there is the huge thing on the other side of the human perceptual wall, all one piece... all one giant Festival where all of that, including our younger selves, our mid-life selves, our old selves are existing simultaneously, and where these people we call dead only passed by our narrow perceptual slat, but are still going on, just on the other side of the wall?

Sisters, let me stress again... we are taking in what we call reality through incredibly narrow apertures, trying to describe everything in three dimensions. There is a likelihood, a HUGE probability... yes, I said *probability*, as in "real building-block of the universe," that we are so so so wrong about everything. Wrong about every thing. Everything. And maybe our grief is just our ignorance. The Fuzz Event is not over. It was never an event. The cat lives on, outside the range of our slat.

Back to the wisdom of Inigo Montoya: *"That word you keep using... I do not think it means what you think it means."*

Well... you may be thinking. "Very clever. And so what? I'm still stuck with my five senses and my three dimensions and the Festival is still over for me on this side of the fence, so it isn't going to matter to me what's going on on the other side."

Well, sisters, yes and no. If nothing is what we think it is and we are 99% probably getting it wrong, what's the point of anything? Well, the point is this radical humility I'm talking about. You don't just decide it's not worth getting out of bed, or that it's a good idea to lie, cheat, and steal since nothing's real anyway. No, sisters, this radical humility, this deep-rooted understanding of the limitations of our synapses, this realization that there are no atomic Legos and therefore no Legoland of matter... *All* of this is an invitation to the Sacred. It is an invitation to create and inhabit sacred space... because that is what is going on just on the other side of the wall, and we know it from the glimpses we catch. And when we live a sacred life, we are bringing that other side over to us as much as we can. And that is no small thing, sisters.

And I know that when Sister Carolyn says something about living a sacred life, it's like nails on a chalkboard to most of you. I know you. I do. But just wait a minute, because a sacred life doesn't mean becoming a nun in some patriarchal religion and waiting for heaven, or climbing up on a mountain and transcending it all because nothing is real anyway. And it doesn't mean sacrifice and deprivation.

No, sisters. In the Lesbian Tent Revival, we take the Michigan Festival as our model and we understand living the sacred life to be one of preoccupation with ritual. And you do know that nearly everything at this Festival is ritual, right? The bell when they open the gates, the Butch Strut, Burrito Night... the torches on Sunday night, the chanting at the Healing Circle. Right down to the Cheezeball Contest. Which is also a radical ritual and subversive repudiation of the male pornographic appropriation of our mammary glands... Yes, sisters, ritual!—*intentional* actions, often repeated, with sacred meaning. And WE, sisters, WE ascribe the meaning.

Preoccupation with ritual. Listen up now. This is all about the end of the Festival. How will we cope with that?

First, we will come to realize we are Flatlanders and Slat-watchers. We are. It's arrogant to think that there are only three dimensions and it's insane to think that our tiny little eye holes and our ear holes can comprehend the universe. So the first thing is this Radical Humility that is going to open up all kinds of space for what we don't know, for forces we can't see, for possibilities of alternate universes we might connect with. So that's the first step.

If Inigo were here, he might say, *"'End of Festival.' Hmm. This phrase you keep using... I do not think it means what you think it does."*

The next step after Radical Humility is the commitment to live a sacred lesbian life. Sisters, that is the only intelligent thing to do when you realize that the material world is not Legoland. And how do we do that?

We become preoccupied with ritual. Ritual that we create, that reflects what we want to see happen, that reflects and projects the world we want to live in. Rituals of healing, rituals of conjuring, rituals of banishing. Ritual saturated in meaning that we give it. And what does it mean to be preoccupied with ritual? It means that our rituals, like Michfest, will come to engross or absorb all our attention—or as much of it as possible— to the exclusion of other thoughts.

We create sacred space that is VISIBLE, sisters, VISIBLE in our homes. Call it an altar. Call it a meditation corner. Call it a pleasure palace. Call it anything you like, or nothing at all, but make it visible and make it sacred. Hang your home with Michigan artifacts. Throw knives into the walls, bake nutloaf. Dance. Dance naked. Just keep adding the sacred until it starts to crowd out the non-sacred.

We will not be the mindless or arrogant or pathetic victims of Flatland or Slat-watching anymore. We will be living out from the world we want, because we have internalized that world... the world of Festival. *Preoccupied with ritual*, sisters. That's the Ticket. If Michfest has taught us anything it is the power of preoccupation with ritual. Lesbian and feminist ritual. And the power of co-creating that ritual. Inhabiting it.

And how can I miss you if you won't go away? If we carry on the living ritual that we learned here at Michfest, maybe we won't miss it quite so acutely. Sisters, we are the Festival. Each one of us. We have the power to carry on the tradition. Let us go forth with that commitment to live sacred lesbian and feminist lives, ever more preoccupied with ritual!

Blessed be!

Sermon on Buying the Land

Sisters… This is Sister Carolyn of the Sisterhood of the Sacred Synapse… which is affectionately known as the "Church of Think-for-Your-Own-Damn-Self." This is a global Sisterhood who celebrate the power of the synaptic connection in the brain by committing ourselves to thinking as radically ("all the way to the root") as possible whenever and wherever we can. Because thinking freely is a privilege, a prerogative, and an obligation in patriarchy.

We met in daily Lesbian Tent Revivals at the Michigan Womyn's Music Festival for nine years, and now that Festival is over and we are meeting here online to do some radical collective synapsing in cyberspace.

So… listen up! Here's a quotation for today: *"The struggle against oppression is a struggle of memory against forgetting."* That's by a Czech writer Milan Kundara who lived his life in exile. All right. I know this is cyberspace, but this is important. I want you to say this with me. "The struggle against oppression".... Come on… "the struggle against oppression… is a struggle of memory against forgetting…" Is what? *"A struggle of memory against forgetting."* So what is the struggle against oppression? *"A struggle of memory against forgetting."* All together: *"The struggle against oppression is a struggle of memory against forgetting."* You've probably already forgotten…

So.. and here's another one that goes with it: *"Until the lion learns to write, every story will glorify the hunter."* This is an African proverb.

So, what am I talking about? I am talking about what we need to do as lesbians, as feminists, as women to overcome patriarchy, to keep ourselves alive and sane, to survive and to thrive, and to pass our legacies on to the women coming up behind us. Well, we have to struggle against oppression. It's a good thing that, "Resistance is the secret of joy." Thank you, Alice Walker, for that gem of wisdom. So we have the joy of struggling against our oppression. And what does that look like? It looks like *memory struggling against forgetting.*

And what the hell does that have to do with a damn lion? Well, synapse with me here. *"Until the lion learns to write, every story will glorify the hunter."* That's patriarchy. That's a description of it and it's also a formula for how it works. It's the what *and* the how. The hunter writes the history. And guess what it's about? How great he is and how well he kills lions. And probably how it's a good thing to kill lions. Over and over.

And the hunter does more than that. He builds institutions and monuments to the lion hunts and to his own mighty prowess and to his weapons. And he names streets and cities after the hunters and the killing grounds. He makes art and movies about the hunters. And he invents whole religions to sanctify and fortify the hunter and to make the slaughter into a ritual.

And guess what? That becomes what people remember. When they are curious about lions, they turn to the hunter and his culture and that's where they get their understanding of lions. The hunter controls what is remembered and in doing that, he also controls what gets forgotten, because what is not written, built, celebrated, or commemorated does not get transmitted. And what does not get transmitted gets lost. And the hunter's version of events gets stronger and stronger, and the lion population gets smaller and more endangered. And the mental health of the perpetually-hunted and endangered lion is not all that great either. Can I get a witness?

Sisters. We must engage our mighty synapses to do battle against forgetting. And that means we have to do something that women have historically not been able to do. We have to learn the skills of commemorating, of creating legacies, of establishing memorials. We have to build up visible, material, concrete, solid evidence of who we are, what we did in our life, and what we valued. We have to shore up the dams of memory to hold back the floodwaters of forgetting and ignorance. We have to take our lesbian selves incredibly seriously.

And we have to do that about our beloved Festival. We have to. "Have to." Not "ought to." Not "should want to." Not "need to." We HAVE TO. Not optional. WE HAVE TO. And We is "you and I." *I* have to. *You* have to. WE have to. We have to. Breathe it in, sisters. "We have to." Breathe it in and start dyking up.

Sisters, we have to buy the Land. We *have to* buy the Land. The Land where so many of us came out as lesbians, where we were safe for the first time in our lives, where we learned to love ourselves and each other, where we reclaimed our female bodies and healed our sexuality, where we found our tribe and our identity, where we connected with our authentic spirituality, where we learned to live in nature and lost our fear of dying, where we began healing journeys out of our addictions and compulsions, where we shed so many of our prejudices and our fears, where we experienced true diversity, deep listening, and respectful communication, and where we found peace, joy, hope, bliss, inspiration, truth and knowledge.

Yes, sisters. We have to buy the Land in order to protect it. We have to buy it and put it in the hands of a legal entity that can protect and steward it into the future. It's going to be a non-profit organization that will hold the land in trust for the benefit of our community, for girls and for women.

The organization is called We Want the Land and they have a Facebook group, and if you join that group you can download all kinds of information about who they are... board members, advisory board, etc. and what they are doing and how they are doing it... so I'm not going to go into that here. We Want the Land. Type it in on Facebook and join up. They got some powerful, powerful women on board, and they are in touch with Lisa Vogel, the owner of the Land, about everything they are doing. The point is: Get on the email list. Get in the loop. There are more than three thousand women on there now. Get on there, sisters. Sign up.

172

Nobody is going to be asked to give money until all of the paperwork is available. Full transparency. And, sisters, you know you need to read all that before you give. Accountability. You got to be accountable to yourself first and foremost.

But that is the business. Let's get back to the Tent Revival perspective. Let's get back to the *"The struggle against oppression is a struggle of memory against forgetting."* Let's get back to how, until the lion learns to write, every story will glorify the hunter.

So the lion has to learn to write. And the Michfest lesbians have to learn how to commemorate ourselves, perpetuate our historical landmarks, protect our sacred lands. The Land is our record.

We were not taught how to do that, as women or as lesbians. It has only been in Sister Carolyn's lifetime we have had a National Museum of Women in the Arts, a Women's Rights National Park, a National Women's Hall of Fame… or the LPGA or the WNBA for that matter. We're still just in the study-up-and-think-about-it phase of building a National Museum of Women's History. Why? Because of our oppression. It takes certain things to be able to commemorate one's histories and celebrate one's battles. For starts, money. And women were often not allowed to work, not allowed the education that would gain us entrance into money-making professions. We often had to turn our money over to husbands, could not inherit, and so on.

But it also takes political clout. Without the vote, it would have been tough to swing that national park in our name. It takes movements. The Women's Liberation Movement. The Lesbian-Feminist Movement. The Lesbian Separatist Movement. The great movements of People of Color of the 1960's that enabled Women of Color to organize around issues of race and gender.

Lesbians have historically survived by passing as heterosexual, by keeping our heads down, by going off on our own where nobody would notice us and nobody could harass us. That's how the Festival started... thousands of lesbians heading out to a 651.2-acre clump of woods in the middle of Michigan farmlands.

All right, sisters, listen up. Do you know the names Monique Wittig and Sande Zeig? Well, you should. They are Saints of the Lesbian Tent Revival. Powerful Sisters of the Sacred Synapse. They were lovers and companions, and they were in cahoots as Mary Daly would say. And they wrote a terribly important book called *Lesbian Peoples: Material for a Dictionary.*

Why is this so important?

Because this can save your life. I mean it. Saint Monique Wittig once said, "Failing to remember, invent." but, of course, she said it in French. She was a French writer. And then she walked her talk, sisters. She walked her talk. She started to invent. She and Saint Sande Zeig began to invent the ancient lesbian history we so desperately need and have never had. And they put it all in the book *Lesbian Peoples*, and it is brilliant and life-saving.

They look at history from a lesbian and feminist perspective, and they invent a past and they invent a future. And these inventions have a truth to them. Sisters, they have a truth that can be more valuable than all the documentation of patriarchal history.

So listen up. They wrote their book in 1976. And they say that this was the beginning of the Glorious Era. The Glorious Era is the age when lesbians flourished and lesbian culture flowered. And here is what they write about the beginning of the Glorious Era:

> *"After harmony had been destroyed in the terrestrial garden, the end of the Golden Age followed. And things have gone from bad to worse. After the Golden Age came the Silver Age... after the Silver Age came the Bronze Age, and after the Bronze Age came the most terrible of all, the origin of chaos, the Iron Age. With this last age there came numerous dark ages to darken it even more, casting the greatest confusion over what for too long a time has been called history... The lesbian peoples do not hold themselves responsible for the confusions, contradictions, incoherences of that history. We have now entered the Glorious Age. This was not achieved without difficulty."*

But sisters, it *was* achieved. They heralded 1976 as the beginning of that Glorious Age and that was the year that the Michigan Womyn's Music Festival was founded. It was a testament to the Glorious Age of lesbians.

Sadly this flowering of lesbian feminist culture, this Glorious Age, was short-lived and only experienced in the West. But it happened. We have the art, the music, the books, the poems, the plays, the incredible history of bookstores and festivals and collectives and women's lands to remember it by. And for forty years the Michigan Womyn's Music Festival conjured up that Glorious Age in the flesh for one week in the Michigan woods. The Glorious Age barely lasted a decade, but the Festival ENSHRINED it, sisters… ENSHRINED it. And now it is up to us to enshrine that enshrinement. Because that Glorious Age was real, it happened. Never forget that.

I am reminded of a lyric from the musical *Camelot*:

> *Don't let it be forgot*
> *That once there was a spot*
> *For one brief shining moment*
> *That was known as Camelot'*

Except that Camelot was a myth. The Michigan Womyn's Music Festival was not.

We must buy the land to remember the Glorious Age. The patriarchy loves to preserve historical sites in Greece and Rome, because it was the so-called beginning of white Western so-called civilization. These were, of course, cultures where the women were owned by men with almost no rights, where people were taken captive and then bought and sold to perform unpaid labor, where children were routinely and legally raped. People go to these sites and walk among the ruins and remember things that never were real. Sisters, we must buy this Land where there are no ruins. Where there are the ferns, the oak trees... ferns that are the descendents of the ones we camped among, oak trees that are perhaps the same ones we sat under. We must buy this Land that has no ruins, but is filled with the life we celebrated and lived with symbiotically for those forty summers. And people will walk those paths where there are no ruins and remember a history that was real. They will remember the Glorious Age.

I think of a quotation by Andy Warhol, "I think that having land and not ruining it is the most beautiful art that anybody could ever want to own."

Sisters we must buy this historical site.

This Land... our Land has the ashes of hundreds of women, of lesbians... of "companion lovers" as Saint Wittig and Saint Zeig would call us. It is a sacred burial ground.

Sisters, we must buy this sacred burial ground.

But it is also a battlefield. It is place where we came and struggled individually and collectively to overcome the internalized enemy: the patriarchal voices of homophobia, misogyny, racism, classism, ageism, ableism, adultism, anti-Semitism. It is a place where many of us did battle with our own compulsions and addictions. And it is a place where we won. Over and over, year after year, sisters... we won. We kicked out the enemy. We reclaimed. We integrated our split-off selves, our horrific memories. We healed.

We were in a place that could hold our victorious selves, in a place that could see and celebrate that victory. We fought hand-to-hand sometimes alone in our tents, or sometimes in skirmishes with our sisters, or in entire battalions with the army of women at Festival. And we won. Time and time again, we won. Because we had established a beachhead of those 650 acres.

What is a beachhead? It is "a defended position on a beach taken from the enemy by landing forces, from which an attack can be launched." We took that land, those acres from the patriarchy. We landed forces there, and we built a city for one week every summer from which our individual and collective attacks could be launched. And when we went home, we took a tiny piece of that beachhead with us. It was tiny, but many of us found it was large enough to hold our ground for another year.

We must buy this beachhead, this battlefield. We must buy this war memorial.

And sisters, the Land was a sanctuary, a place of refuge in times of trouble. And we know the patriarchy is a perpetual time of trouble... for everyone, but especially for dykes. We know this. And many of us came to the Land for that blessed week of sanctuary. We came as members of an endangered species. We came from the violence of childhoods of captivity and torture, young adulthoods of being prey on perpetual hunting grounds of sexual predation. We came as mothers, frantic to nurture, protect and provide for children in a

178

sadistically indifferent, child-hating culture. We came as lesbian artists in a world that reflected back to us that our work—our precious and hard-won visions—were insignificant, juvenile, irrelevant and useless. As artists, we came from a world that starved us for our pains.

We came as disabled warriors… wounded and then stigmatized and blamed for our wounds, by the culture that had inflicted or exacerbated them. We came as crones, our wisdom dismissed and our longevity ridiculed, punished with poverty for lives of generosity and unselfed love for our sisters. We came from wars, literal wars, from the siege of organized patriarchal religions, from governments that oppressed us in our name, from medical institutions that had labeled us crazy, misdiagnosed, and misprescribed for us. We came in desperate need of those seven days of sanctuary. And we found that refuge. And we found refuges within our refuge. Women of Color had their own sanctuary. Deaf women had their own camping. Jewish women had their own tent. Women in recovery had their own meetings. Disabled women had their own camping area. The girls had their own area and programming. The boys had their own camp. The women who wanted judgment-free zones for "loud and rowdy" camping had their own area.

We have to buy this sanctuary.

And sisters, the Land was a sacred site of mystical healing. It was a place where we could feel the spirits of our lesbian ancestors—certainly the spirits of the women whose ashes were on the Land, but also the spirits before them. We felt the spirits of the African women whose voices came through the drums, the music, the dancing from that culture. We felt the heritage of Sappho in the poetry that celebrated lesbian courage and passion. The voices of so many ancestors were all collected at the Goldenrod booth, in the songs of women, and at the People Called Women Bookstore booth. We gathered in workshops to commemorate the deaths of Andrea Dworkin, Joanna Russ, Mary Daly, Adrienne Rich, Julia Penelope... and so many more. The spirits of the witches were felt in the Dianic Wiccan rituals of the Land, and the spirits of the legendary Amazons stood guardian over our week. And we were healed. We were healed in the Oasis, where we did recovery work and could unburden ourselves to women who would listen with compassion and in sisterhood. We were healed in the Womb where herbs and Western medicine and chiropractic and allopathic all came together in peace, not competition, for the unique needs of each sister.

We came to the healing circle, to the labyrinths, to the workshops. We healed in the silliness and in the sacredness. We healed in the mosh pits and we healed in the Sacred Singing. We healed on the massage tables and around the campfires. Sisters, we healed. And we healed in the healthy food that we all joked about and still joke about. And our laughter healed us. We healed in the ferns, and in each others' arms. We healed in Workerville, and in the Craft Area. We healed running and marching in the parades and dancing under the August sky. Sisters, the Land is a place of sacred healing and it must remain a place where women can come and make sacred pilgrimages. It is our home.

We must buy this site of miraculous healings, this place of pilgrimage.

Sisters, we have to. You have to. I have to. Not optional. It is a privilege, a prerogative and an obligation to preserve this land in perpetuity for ourselves and for our sisters.

We must never forget what we built in this time and in this place.

Blessed be!

Sermon on Confronting

You know, sisters, they say there is no such thing as courage... It's really just about wanting something more than you fear your fears. I believe that is true. And I believe that we can cultivate courage just by focusing on a thing that we want more.

So today I am going to talk about something that nearly everybody fears, and how to get past that with something nearly everybody wants. Hopefully, it is going to change everybody's life. That's the hope. For the better.

What is that thing we all fear? Or that most of us fear? Confronting people.

So here's how my brain works on the subject of confrontation...

Let's say I am standing in line for something, in a crowd. Let's say that suddenly, I feel someone standing on my foot. Hard. So here is my brain:

1) Ouch!
2) Is this really what I think it is? Is someone actually standing on my foot...? Am I sure I'm not just making it up?
3) Well, how bad is it, really? I'm sure they will move soon.
4) Can I inch my foot out from under without them noticing? *Because I don't want to embarrass them about standing on my foot.* (Seriously. I think that way.)

5) Can I create a distraction and then jerk my foot away?

6) Is anyone else noticing what's happening to me?

7) Why me? Why today?

8) Oh, Goddess, look at me...! I'm such a wimp! I can't even tell someone to get off my foot... What is wrong with me?

9) Oh, thank god! My foot is going numb. Good. See... I knew it would be all right. Just wait long enough, and most things will sort themselves out.

You think I am exaggerating? I'm not. That's pretty much the process. Why?

Because Sister Carolyn does not like to confront people. Ever. About anything. She will run down every single other option, including some truly disastrous ones, before she will confront.

Harmless, right? Her business, as long as her foot stays numb... right?

Wrong. Wrong-wrong-wrong. Sisters, not confronting is like metaphysical termites. You don't usually see them, because they're so small... and then one day the foundation of your home collapses.

Not confronting can have devastating outcomes. How do I know this? It just happened to me this spring.

In a nutshell, I had a friend die recently. I was unable to be present for her the last eighteen months of her dying from cancer. We did not have contact. Why? What happened?

Well… It's too long a story and too personal of one to tell here, but the truth of it was that I had been afraid to confront her for the entire fourteen years of our friendship. She scared me. Each time something would come up that I was not comfortable with, I would tell myself, "Well, she lives on the other coast, and we rarely see each other… so let it go." Or, "I've seen her do this to other people, to everyone around her, in fact, and they never confront, so I'm not going to be the one." Or "She has been so incredibly generous toward me and toward my art… is this really that important?" And of course, the usual analysis of her painful childhood, the fact she grew up in a different socio-economic culture… blah blah blah.

Lots of excuses for why I didn't confront, but the real reason was I was afraid. I was afraid it would not go well. I was afraid that she would hurt me. I knew she wasn't going to do anything physical, or even raise her voice, but I was afraid that she would say something devastating to me personally. Something shaming. Something that would throw it back on me, point out my defects, bring up a time when I did such-and-such to her… That she would remind me of how much she had done for me and how little I could do for her. I would feel rejected, insulted, shamed, inferior, ungrateful. I would suddenly see how little she thought of me.

Sometimes my fear of confronting is based on ignorance: I don't know the person very well, so they could do anything. But in this case it was based on knowledge. My friend had a history of not apologizing. She also did not ask for things. She tended to bark orders. She issued commands. She gave generously, but acted as if her generosity had entitled her. I never saw her interrogate her actions or perspectives.

Good reasons not to confront, yes? No. The reason for confronting is to establish our boundaries. We confront to let folks know they have stepped over them. How they respond is not our business. At least not where a friendship is concerned... not where having an authentic relationship is the goal.

BUT... I was afraid. I chose not to confront. For fourteen solid years I did not confront. But I did not forget, either. I was stockpiling each and every boundary violation, each and every passive aggressive power play. I had a frickin' warehouse of resentments. And all this time, my fear of her was growing. Because that's what fear does when we don't confront.

And then she became terminally ill. She was needing her friends in a way that she had never needed us before. And, of course, she was not asking. She was leaning into her entitlement, which was her method of operating. She was calling in her favors. And suddenly, her entitlement warehouse ran smack into my warehouse of resentments. I did not step up the way she wanted me to, and she did everything I had always been afraid she would do: she took my inventory, shamed and insulted me. Her points about me had enough validity to hurt badly. I was actually traumatized by her communication with me. She may have been traumatized by my response to her very great need.

And I withdrew. Completely. Everything I could think of to say and do appeared to me as if it would end up on a dead-end street... including admitting that everything was my fault and that I was a terrible person... yes, even that. All those years of not confronting had painted me into a corner, and I now found myself in a place where every interaction I could imagine led to a scenario that was unmanageable.

And here let me say that my friend was a complicated woman, as am I. She was funny, and compassionate... deeply compassionate. She was creative and playful, generous, loyal... really loyal. She was dear. Often childlike... and smart as a whip. And then there was this very ugly, bullying side. She was, like me—like most of us—a mixed bag. Damage and privilege living side-by-side. Grandiosity and insecurity sharing the same roof in an unstable alliance.

So... she was in the fight of her life and scared, really scared. She could not control the cancer. She had a tendency to control everything, big and little... and here was the thing she most needed to control, and she could not. She could not buy her way out of cancer. And here was me... a woman for whom she had done so much... and I could not be there. I could not even contact her.

And before you judge me too harshly, I want to say that I got a lot of help with the situation. I talked to a lot of friends, and I worked especially closely with my sponsor in Alanon. Over those 18 months, I questioned my choices constantly. I made an uneasy and painful peace with those choices... BUT I wish that I had not ended up in a place where the choice that was healthy for me was so painful for both of us. I don't regret my choice, but I regret the behaviors that led to my having to make it.

And that behavior was my failure to confront.

What if I had confronted my friend in the early years, when we were getting to know each other? Well, honestly, I strongly suspect it would not have gone well, and that our budding friendship may have been aborted. But I don't know that for sure. Maybe that would have happened and I would have missed the fourteen years of experiences with her... *or* maybe a conversation would have happened. Maybe we would have entered some kind of process. Maybe we both would have surprised each other and ourselves with our capacity for change. But one thing I am pretty sure of: I would not have the pain that I have now about the end.

This business of not confronting, not speaking up... well, it's not a magic trick and it's not a shortcut. The issues don't just go away because you choose not to confront. They get split off and hidden.

When we choose not to confront, there is the part of us that we show to our friend, and then there is this growing, secret part that is unhappy with some behavior or behaviors and that is afraid to confront. So now there are two parts to us: the face we show and the keeper of resentments. And as the years go by and the not-confronting piles up, the relationship becomes more and more of a performance and the keeper of resentments becomes more and more our truth about the friendship. It's like every time something happens that we don't confront, we move a little piece of ourselves away from the friendship and give it to the keeper of resentments.

And then, one day, something happens... the straw that breaks the camel's back... and we find that we are speaking with the voice of the keeper of resentments. We have moved ourselves over entirely. The resentments have become our greater truth. And our abandoned friend feels confused and betrayed. They genuinely do not know what has happened. We seem to have changed overnight for no reason, or for a trivial reason... because we never showed them our secret self. And we may also find ourselves surprised to feel so hard-hearted and detached all of a sudden.

And here is the sad horror of the whole thing: Often that turning point—that critical mass of resentments—happens when our friend is down, when something has weakened her, when she is now vulnerable. Suddenly we may be less afraid of her. And that is when the keeper of resentments will make her move... even though we may not be conscious of our motive. When we stockpile resentments, we forfeit control over when and where and how things will blow up.

I was afraid of my friend, because she definitely could bully. I had seen her do it. But I am afraid to confront a lot of things with a lot of people. It's in my wiring. It just always seems easier and better for everyone, including me, not to say anything. I don't like to look at how much fear informs my behavior. Nobody likes to know they are a coward. I prefer to focus on the things the other person does that scare me.

Anyway, I didn't show up for the end of my friend's life, but honestly, I had not been showing up for a long time before that.

People like me who have a habit of not confronting, also have a string of relationships that suddenly blew up or just disappeared. People we really loved, really knew, really did significant work with... and poof, suddenly they are gone. And we are hurt or puzzled, but mostly, we are feeling the weight of those secret resentments... so what the hell... or even good riddance... and we conclude that people are scary. They just disappear. Better to invest in a garden, a cat, a hobby. But people...? Poof. Gone.

And here's the thing. When we don't confront, eventually EVERYBODY BECOMES EXPENDIBLE. I'm going to say that again, because it's so important: If you don't confront, EVERYBODY, SOONER OR LATER, BECOMES EXPENDIBLE. Yeah. And it's not them. It's us. It's us not confronting.

And, sisters, we're getting down to it now, because in a world where we are feeling that everybody is expendable, you know that, sooner or later, we're going to feel that way about ourselves, too. I have my go-rounds with suicidal thoughts. And I am only just now realizing how linked that is to my failure to confront things, and the repeated expendability of people I love.

I can't tell you how much pain this death caused me. And I can't tell you how much pain I feel when I realize that all these people who have disappeared out of my life might still be here if I had just understood and acted on my obligation to confront them.

So here's that courage part: The next time you're afraid to confront, try to shift over to that part where you want something greater than you fear the fear. Do you want to lose the friendship altogether? Do you want to be like me... unable to show up when this friend is in the fight of her life? Focus on wanting the friendship and wanting to be a friend. Focus on wanting that more than you fear the confrontation or its outcome.

So... confronting. As a culture, we're not good at it. Systems of power do not stay in place because people are taught to confront them. There is a political and cultural dimension to our silences.

So let's get some tools for breaking those silences.

Let's get some technique. You know, like we did with sex.

Okay... first learn to identify that feeling in your gut... that little electric shock when somebody comes over your fence without your permission.

And then learn to identify that weird hazy thinking like what I talked about at the beginning of this sermon... all the different ways NOT to confront someone standing on my foot.

190

And then—and this is key!—learn to say these magic words: "Right now I am CHOOSING not to confront this." Sisters, that's a really important step. To realize and to name the fact that we are making a choice when we don't confront. Even if you change nothing else, doing that one little step will begin to change you. I promise. So do that. Say, "Oh, look, they did something I'm not comfortable with and right now I am CHOOSING not to confront. Well, what do you know?" This creates the possibility of doing something different. A next step might be to consider options. Just to *consider*.

And then, if you can, change the script. Confront if you can.

And what does that sound like?

"I" statements, not "you" statements. Say that you are uncomfortable and tell them what they did that caused you to feel uncomfortable, and explain why their choice or behavior is uncomfortable for you. Take a little stop there. Maybe they will be accountable just hearing that. Maybe you need to go further and tell them what you need them to do in order to feel comfortable with them. And sometimes you need to go even further and spell out the consequences, if they can't be accountable.

Sometimes confronting in the moment is a great thing, and sometimes it's not. If not, or if you didn't even realize you needed to confront until later... then tell them there is something you need to talk to them about and work *with* them to find a time and place to have that conversation. It should be convenient for both of you.

Get feedback. Before, if you can, and definitely after. Confronting is hard, and if you don't do it often, it's helpful to hear what trusted friends have to say. I don't think confrontations should be done by email. Too easy for them to speed-read them in the middle of a bunch of business email and fire back some brusque push-back answer. On the other hand, writing a letter can give them time to think and consider. There's no button to push. They have more choice over when they will open it and read it. Or talking on the phone, where it's not so impersonal and where the nuances of tone are not lost.

I don't have a lot to say about this… except that I am 65 years old, and I have lived a huge life. And if I had to look at my single biggest regret, I would say it was this: I allowed my fears to keep me from confronting the people I cared about.

So, sisters, let's all be better at this. We really need each other. And it will be worth it.

Blessed be.

Sermon on Holding Contradiction

Sisters, we are living in a time where there is a tremendous pull to see the world as good or evil. I know it. You know it. But, sisters, when we do that, we become so easy to lead… or rather, mislead. And we wildly cut off our synaptic pathways. It's like posting a ton of "do not enter" signs all over our brain. One of the greatest threats to our freedom is this limiting of our own synapses.

I think of that line in *Jaws*… when the character Brody is out on a boat and he sees the shark for the first time, and he backs into the cabin where Quint is and says, "We're gonna need a bigger boat." Sisters, with what's menacing this country now, we are gonna need a bigger synaptic boat. I mean it.

And this is a hard subject. I know it is. Black-and-white thinking simplifies things. It makes it easier for large numbers of people to do things… which can be good and bad at the same time. We are all overworked, stressed by the pace of the world. The temptation to think in terms of black-and-white, good-and-evil is great.

But, Sisters, resist it. Trust yourself to think better when you keep those synaptic pathways, all of them, open.

So Sisters, we're going to do a little brain-stretching today. Because it's important. It's important to thinking radically. Are you ready to stretch your brains… ? Are you willing to feel the burn…? All right. So, here we go:

First, let's do a little test…

How many of you can pick up an adorable little puppy and cuddle her and at the same time be unhappy that she peed on you? In other words, how many of you feel that you don't have to love the pee to love the puppy? And you don't have to hate the puppy because you hate the pee…?

Okay. Well, that's good.

Well, how about your next door neighbor who helped you dig out your car last winter and loaned you a ladder to get the ice dams off your roof… but who has a "one-man-one-woman" sticker on the back of his truck? Do you have to avoid asking him for help again? Or do you need to tell yourself he bought the truck used and the sticker was already there, and he has no idea what it means? Do you have to cut him off socially or pretend not to know an inconvenient truth about his political views?

Okay… getting tougher now.

So how about your favorite candidate…? A person who is right on so many of the issues, but then you find out that they voted in favor of a bill that hugely offends you… because it's totally wrong, duh. Do you need to tell yourself it must have been an offensive amendment tacked on by his or her opponents at the last minute in an effort to tank the bill, but your candidate still voted in favor because the issues in the original bill outweighed the one offensive one? Or do you tell yourself that this candidate only pretends to be progressive and that one offensive issue reveals the true venality underlying all his or her posing to care about x-y-z issues?

Well… let's bring the war home…

Your partner is a funny and well-intentioned person and really awesome at fixing things and great at her job… and she drinks too much and has been abusive under the influence. AND before you all start yelling at me… I am *not* talking about not confronting. I'm *not* talking about not holding her accountable. I'm *not* talking about not reporting to the police if there is danger to you. I'm *not* talking about not leaving. I'm *not* talking about inaction, because you know me better than that. And you all know you have a right and an obligation to protect yourself from abuse.

But what I am talking about is how you *think* of that person, especially over time. Do you need to overlook or deny the drinking and write off the offenses, because she didn't know what she was doing? Or do you need to edit out all the ways she is a truly wonderful woman? Do you need to trash all the memories of the good times? Can you hold both in mind at the same time? Whatever choices you made for your own safety and welfare—and you know you have to make those, can you still hold those two aspects, Dr. Jekyll and Mr. Hyde, in your mind at the same time?

Yeah, see, this is getting hard. And still bringing the war home, literally…

You are a huge activist and you do a lot of anti-capitalist activism... And you have a 401K at work and it is invested in a mutual fund that includes oil companies, price gouging pharmaceutical companies, etc. And you know that nearly every single company in your portfolio makes money from doing business with the military. They are the largest single contractor in the country. Even if you are doing socially responsible investing, trust me, your companies are still most likely making some kind of profit from the military. So... Do you have to forget about what your money is supporting? Or do you have to retreat from your activism because you feel like a hypocrite? Can you keep your 401K and still show up to fight against Citizens United or against the latest war?

OR...

There is some artist whose work has meant so much to you... you love her art. It's brilliant. Let's say Virginia Woolf... and then you discover that she sexually molested her niece... which, according to said niece, she did. Do you never read her writing again, never cite her again... throw out the books? Or do you call the niece a little liar. And we could say this for Anne Sexton. She was sexually abusing her daughter while she was writing a play about a daughter being sexually abused. And I could go on... It's kind of easy for some of us to boycott Woody Allen movies, but if we apply that same criteria to women writers, it gets a little more painful, and little tougher.

So… Let's keep all of these in mind… Because today our topic is holding contradictions. Why is it that the puppy was easy for us, but some of the others were not?

Well, I'll tell you… The contradictions in the puppy were not that antithetical. The puppy can't help being adorable and can't help peeing. It's a puppy, for goddess' sake. But when we get to your girlfriend or the famous feminist author, we expect much more and we need them to be accountable. And when we are talking about the policies of a political candidate, we may be talking about our core values.

Short digression here… So just stick a pin in the "holding contradiction" thing for a minute. We're coming back to it, I promise.

So, Sister Carolyn reads a lot about suicide. She's lost a number of friends. She tries to understand it… And it's interesting what they have found about it. People take their lives because they are suffering. Okay, that's pretty obvious. And that suffering can be from grief, or from physical pain, or loss of quality of living… lots of reasons. But one of the biggest is from losing a sense of who they are. This is called an "existential crisis." Wikipedia calls it "the moment at which an individual questions the very foundations of their life: whether this life has any meaning, purpose, or value." One of the big reasons why people kill themselves is because they are having an existential crisis. Inspector Javert in *Les Miz* jumps into the river and drowns himself when his whole notion of justice and life purpose is overturned.

In the Great Depression where so many folks lost all their money practically overnight, there were lots of stories of folks jumping off of buildings and so on... but these folks hadn't even been poor yet. They still had fridges full of food, even second homes. Most of them might not feel the pinch for months or even years. Their losses were still on paper. They jumped because they didn't know who they could be without their wealth. They could not see themselves working as a busboy or taking the subway to work. They wouldn't be themselves anymore. They were having an existential crisis.

Sometimes survivors take our lives, because we confront abuse in our families and we are met with denial and rejection... and we have, sadly, not been able to find alternative families or support systems outside that family of birth. We may know intellectually that we are sane and we are right, but when it feels like everyone in the world is saying we are wrong or evil or deluded, we can have an existential crisis. Are we who we think we are... or are we who they say we are? This is why it's so important to handpick our support systems.

Anyway, the point is that a sense of self is pretty critical to living. We need to know who we are. And we need to believe in who we are. And who we are is a bundle of things... our memories, our dreams, our failures, our experiences, our relationships, our achievements, how others see us, ... and our values. Especially our values. Values are kind of like geographical coordinates. They help us locate ourselves. Latitude X and longitude Y. And they help other people locate us, too. And we can locate them. And these coordinates give us place, community with others, qualities, and character. Our values keep us safe, define our goals, help us make choices. Our values are a huge part of who we are.

When we become unsure about our core values, we become unsure about who we are… and that is the dreaded existential crisis. It is authentically life-threatening. Which is why most folks put up such a fierce fight for our values.

So… hold that thought: You are your values.

And so now let's get back to the subject of this sermon: holding contradiction.

Holding contradiction can feel like a terrible, wishy-washy, "all truths are subjective" type of thing. It can feel like we are being asked to be complicit. It can feel like a direct attack or a subtle undermining of our core values… like a push over the edge of the existential cliff.

WELL ISN'T IT??

Yes and no. See what I did there? Holding contradiction…

The world is really complex and very few things are completely black and white. And even when they are… the solutions for dealing with them may not be so black-and-white. Many solutions are all about "hold your nose and vote." Or… "detach with love." Or "do what you need to do, but don't go into denial about anything while you do it… for good or bad."

One of the characteristics of post-traumatic stress disorder, otherwise known as PTSD, is black-and-white thinking. You are either a friend or an enemy. I can trust you completely or not at all. This is right and that is wrong. Completely. Agree with me or I can't have you in my bed, my life, my place of employment, my Facebook page, my whatever.

Why is black-and-white thinking part of PTSD? Because trauma results in fight, flight, freak, or freeze. Response to trauma does not involve the cortex. It does not involve complex problem-solving, alternative perspectives, looking at all the options, gathering feedback, informed decisions, strategic alliances, compromise. It's primitive, and it comes from a primitive part of the brain that is perceiving a situation as life-threatening. And often, especially in childhood, it is.

So there is the immediate response in the moment, and in the heat of that moment, there is synaptic soldering going on... links are being forged between the life-threatening stimuli and the trauma response... links that will determine your response next time you encounter similar stimuli. If the last time you heard a door bang open, it was followed by an act of violence, the sound of that door banging—or any door banging—or anything that sounds remotely like a door banging will elicit a trauma response.

Black-and-white. No door sound = good. Door banging sound = bad. But in the real world, doors bang. Good people come through doors that bang. Children especially bang doors. To avoid the door bang, we would probably need to go live in a place where everyone was camping in tents.

What do we do when we have these hard-wired, black-and-white trauma responses? Well… we can try to minimize being restimulated. The go-live-in-a-tent-in-the-woods thing. More about that later. Or we can try to work our way through the PTSD, or trauma responses. We can learn to integrate the experience of the trauma… or "unfreeze it," as they say, so that it's not always with us as if it's happening now. We can move it out of the part of the brain that stored it and get it filed somewhere else in the brain, somewhere not so primitive, where we begin to experience it as something that happened in the past. And then we can start to involve the cortex in figuring out whether or not the sound we are hearing is something that should alarm us. We can begin to modify our behaviors, make choices, observe our process and articulate it. We can synapse more effectively around being triggered by a reminder of a traumatic event.

So… that's the theory about black-and-white thinking with trauma. And why am I telling you this? Because our values can be forged in trauma. Okay, work with me… Let's say puppy pee had flesh-eating properties, and that you have had a trauma association from being peed on by a puppy and having your flesh eaten. You probably dropped or threw or ran away from the puppy as soon as she peed on you. Whatever warm fuzzy feelings you had for the cute little puppy disappeared in that instant of flesh-eating agony. You would never be tricked by those big brown eyes or that cute little yelp again. Your emotions will never betray you into picking up a puppy again. You learn to harden your heart against cute-puppy-face.

So, in the interests of "never again," you walk away from the puppy—all puppies. All the time. And you steer clear of those people who have puppies in their homes. The puppies are dangerous and those who love them are crazy. You are uncomfortable around cute puppy calendars, puppy films, Facebook postings about puppies. Maybe you start to avoid kittens, too… just because. You have paid a high price to know what you know about puppies and their piss, and you are not going to lose that knowledge. Core values.

Core values. Central to our sense of who we are. Core values: those things that keep us from having an existential crisis.

So let's think about some religious people for a minute. Orthodox fill-in-the-blank… Christian/Jew/Muslim… or even hardcore atheist. Often these folks avoid anyone who does not share their faith or, in the case of the atheist, lack thereof. One who disagrees with them is apostate or a sinner, or in the case of the atheist, a brainwashed and potentially dangerous fool drinking the koolaid. These folks like to, and even need to be around people who share their religious values. Why wouldn't they? It's exhausting to be around people whose very existence or lifestyle challenges our core values every minute. So who can blame them? Nobody wants friends who take that much work.

Let's think about people who feel passionate about veganism or vegetarianism, who cannot be in the presence of people who are eating meat. Or folks who feel that way about people who use drugs or drink... or use drugs and drink to x-y-z extent.

Life is a constant negotiation. Lesbians, feminists, women, survivors feel our truths—our identities under assault constantly, because they are. We can feel great relief when we are with other lesbians, feminists, women, survivors.... but we can also feel deeply betrayed when these lesbians, feminists, women, survivors introduce values in other areas that challenge us. It's almost like they are a Trojan horse... coming into our community, or our life, or our bedroom like they are an ally, but in reality they are bearing enemy propaganda—or, at least, that is the way we may be perceiving the situation. I am thinking of the so-called sex wars in lesbian community when "sisters" began introducing sadomasochistic sexual practices. So many examples... Some lesbians feel betrayed by lesbians who wear makeup, or who dye their hair, or—in the old days—who had male offspring and insisted on raising them.

So today we are considering and considering deeply the line between resilience and becoming complicit.

Sisters, I cannot tell you where that line is. I negotiate and renegotiate it all day long. I am serious. I used to be very black-and-white, very post-traumatic in my thinking. When I recovered my incest memories at the age of 32, I lost my entire immediate and extended family. And then I went through a devastating experience as a whistleblower in a huge lawsuit against a university. And then I lost my church for being lesbian, and I lost my teaching job for being lesbian. I felt I was betrayed by the medical community when they could not diagnose my Chronic Fatigue Sydrome and kept telling me there was nothing wrong with me. All of these betrayals were deeply traumatic and, as a result, I got very, very black-and-white. Only women were safe. No, change that...! Only lesbians. No, wait...! Only lesbian-feminists are safe. Wait, no...! Only non-religious, lesbian-feminists... Only uncloseted, non-religious, living-off-the-grid lesbian-feminists. And, at one time only uncloseted, non-religious, living-off-the-grid lesbian-feminists who had demonstrated a willingness and a capacity to kill men. Not a huge subset. And guess what? I wasn't feeling any safer.

In fact, as my attempts to find safety got more and more honed, I was feeling more and more vulnerable... because isolation and marginalization can do that to a person. Maybe I wasn't feeling my values challenged by folks with radically different perspectives and experiences, but I was living so far outside of society, like an outlaw, that it was generating paranoia and its own set of vulnerabilities. Also, the folks in my subset were nearly all survivors like me, with active PTSD... so the folks I was relying on for role models and validation were more like a funny house of distorted mirrors. And we were constantly monitoring each other for signs of impurity, of patriarchal viruses. It was, actually, pretty much a dystopian nightmare.

But, what would have happened to me at that time in my life if I had opened myself to Christian lesbians, closeted lesbians... lesbians who enjoyed sadomasochism, lesbians who occasionally resorted to strategies of appeasement, lesbians with males or male children in their lives? Well… at that period of my life, I might have felt that I was wrong. And, at that time in my life, feeling that I might be wrong could have actually killed me. It was that existential crisis thing.

I had to be right. I mean, I *really* had to be right. When your family, your educational institution, your place of employment, your doctor, and your church all tell you that you are wrong, and when you are the *only* one in your corner… you *have* to be right. Really, really right. Maybe even righter than anyone else has ever been right on the whole planet. Right. At all times. Maybe even not go to sleep in case you dream something that might make you wrong. Or make you think you're wrong.

That period of my life was extreme, I admit. But so was my abuse. Most of us struggle with some form of investment in our values, in being right, in protecting ourselves from things that remind of us trauma. Most of us would prefer it when things are black and white. Most of us wish that Virginia Woolf was either a terrible writer or had not abused her niece.

But, thinking about Woolf—here's the thing… What if Virginia Woolf's brilliant writings have helped a survivor understand the patriarchal backdrop to her violation, which helps defuse shame or a false senses of responsibility? What if Virginia Woolf's writing is a powerful, feminist tool for healing from trauma? Should we throw it away because she perpetrated? Can we hold her accountable for that, can we hold our anger and horror over the perpetration and still respect the work?

And I am not sure there is a right or wrong answer. If Woolf was perpetrating in her life, might there not be subtle, toxic, perpetrator-apologist messages sprinkled through her writing? Will we catch them, if they are there? Will they infect us? Can we really treasure the work and not find ourselves giving a pass to Woolf for her behavior? Might we not be safer just putting it down?

I don't have any easy answers about holding complexity, but I know that I lost dozens of friends in the last election because either they or I was struggling with or not even trying to hold complexity. I know that I paid a high price for my years of separatism... even as it gave me many gifts of focus and clarity in my writing. And, on the other hand, I know that I sometimes—often—feel I'm getting morally compromised when I hold complexity.

But sisters, the world is wide. People are complicated. Issues are complicated. Our thinking is massively influenced by conditions and conditioning about which we may not even be aware. Holding complexity, holding contradiction creates a space. One can argue it is a space for perpetration. Maybe. And maybe we can know when that is. I do know this: holding complexity can create space for transformation. That neighbor with the bumper sticker... nothing is going to change him quicker than befriending people in same sex relationships. That might happen if we create the space to act neighborly and accept that this is where he is at, at least in terms of bumper stickers, right now, but we hold the thought that he might not always identify with homophobic notions.

Now, I want to be clear… I'm talking about the neighbor who has been personally helpful but whose truck's rear end is ideologically offensive. That's one thing. It's another thing entirely if that neighbor has expressed hostility or been disrespectful. It's another thing when someone is intimate and abusive. No, you don't hang around and try to change them by example. You take the actions that you need to in order to protect yourself and hold them accountable. But do you need to trash them, to banish them to outer darkness? How do you hold them in thought? How do you talk about them?

Sisters, I have come to my own conclusions about holding complexity. I think it's a good thing for me. I think that it is where I have grown the most. Challenging my boundaries, challenging my values. Sometimes I let something in that I have to move out again. Sometimes I have kept something out that I need to make space for. I'm growing and changing, and circumstances around me are growing and changing. I can be pragmatic without being a sell-out, and I can be idealistic or visionary without tunnel vision. Example: I have strong feelings about marriage as a government institution regulating a private relationship, *and,* sisters, I voted for marriage equality in my state because of the current context where lesbian partners cannot access each others' retirement benefits, and so on. But do I think the government should have jurisdiction over our committed, sexual relationships? No.

I remember a lesbian once told me that people who are judgmental lack confidence in their judgment. I never forgot it. I heard this when I was in the middle of my most PTSD-filled, inventory-taking years. Which is probably why she made the comment to me in the first place.

Yes, I have lacked confidence in my judgment. I have been through years, decades, of seriously lacking that confidence in my own judgment. Examples? I have a long history of being attracted to active addicts... that's a thing that can happen to the brain, a kind of Stockholm Syndrome from growing up with alcoholics. I was deeply religious... also a pretty standard response to trauma and chaos as a child. I chose a career based on me being someone I was not... because I had absolutely no idea who my authentic self was. Hell, yeah, I learned not to trust my own judgment!

But I'm here now. And I've done a lot of work. And I don't need to send everybody out of the room before I enter it. I don't need mental metal detectors for everyone who enters. I feel more and more I can walk into that room and I will know how to take care of myself, no matter who is in it. And I'm actually excited and curious about the folks who don't think like me. Sometimes I make poor judgments, but I don't marry them and I don't die.

Having my values challenged doesn't send me into existential panic anymore. Some of this is the gift of aging, of having some security. But a lot of it has been a slow process of creating that space to hold complexity. "Yes-and." "Yes-and." Over and over. Three steps forward, two steps back.

208

There are a couple of things that I find helpful in holding complexity. The first is understanding addiction as a disease, not a moral failing or a character defect. If you have an aging grandmother with Alzheimers, and you have watched the progression of it, and suddenly one day, she throws her dinner plate across the room in a fit of rage you've never seen before... well, you are probably not going to say, "My grandmother is a violent asshole and I'm just now realizing it." You're also probably not going to say, "Well, that didn't really happen." You're more likely to say, "Her disease has reached a new stage." And the meaning of that incident is not that you have been mistaken in loving her, or that you must now avoid her like the plague. The meaning is more like "New decisions are going to have to be made now, in terms of her care." You can hold in thought that you love her dearly and that she has a disease that has rendered her behaviors dangerously violent.

Well, I work to hold a similar model for alcoholism and drug addiction. The disease model. Substance abuse disorder. Yeah. Learn to say that. Seriously. Folks with substance abuse disorder don't get a pass on the behaviors and I still have to make decisions about the addict's place in my life, but I work to separate who they are in my mind from what I know about addiction as a disease. And I admit, this is not easy, because I didn't really start to educate myself about alcoholism until I was in my 40's. I had a lot of mental habits to undo, and it takes work. It's easy for me to write off everyone who drinks and behaves badly as a selfish asshole. But I am diminished by that kind of thinking. I am having to edit out the incredible gifts of these friends and family members. It does not serve me to do that.

So that is one tool: See addiction as a disease. It really helps with the black-and-white.

And the second tool is understanding that life is all about process. I may need to upload some black-and-white thinking to find the courage to confront someone, or to fire them, or to detach from them right now, or to get a restraining order today. But I can know, even as I am raging about how awful they are, that this is just what I am thinking today. It may not be how I need to think tomorrow. It may be helpful today, right now for me. And tomorrow it may no longer be helpful. It may be wrong for me tomorrow. I may need some cooling off, some time, some space, some healing. But I do know that holding complexity is where I grow. I keep that in mind as a goal.

The third thing is to understand that an analysis is not a judgment, and that an analysis does not necessarily need to lead to a judgment. And just because you have an analysis, that does not mean you are entitled to make a judgment.

I can have an analysis about why women shave body hair and men don't. That does not mean that I need to have a judgment about women who shave their legs or their pubis or their armpits. And it certainly does not mean that I have an obligation or an entitlement to interpret their choices for them. *And* the corollary of this is that, just because I am not judging someone, I don't have to forgo my analysis. I don't have to tell myself that the urge to remove body hair is a mystical urge of all normal females rooted in their biology, just because I am not judging the woman. I don't have to say that all females are born with a pink bow and a razor in their tiny fist. I can know what I know culturally, historically, or even personally about someone. I am entitled to my analysis. But I am not entitled to judge, unless I find myself on a literal jury in a court case. Then I am entitled to judge.

I can't tell you how helpful this little semantic separation is in terms of holding complexity, and also in holding onto friendships. I know that my friends who are vegan have profound and complex analyses of the eating of meat. I probably would agree with it. *And* I am eternally grateful they don't judge me. Or, at least, I don't have to hear about it.

Holding complexity is not to be confused with "all truths are equally valid." As Holocaust historian Deborah Lipstadt said, *"Sometimes... we grow up thinking, oh, everything should be open to debate, and everything should be open to question, and there are always two sides to every story, and the enlightened view is to keep your mind open to two sides to every story. Well, there aren't two sides to every story. The Holocaust happened. Slavery happened. Elvis is dead."*

Holding complexity is not about thinking that the neighbor is correct in his homophobia or that it is right for him to hold those views, just as it is right for you to hold yours. Holding complexity is understanding the significance of his prejudice and of his bumper sticker, understanding their potential danger to you, and holding this danger in thought with an appreciation of his helpfulness during the ice storm, and taking both of these opposite ideas and using them to negotiate your choices for going forward in your interactions with him.

Holding complexity is mental yoga. It creates space. What comes into that space can be peace, humility, wisdom, spirituality. And sometimes answers get forged in those spaces, answers that our frightened or egotistical minds could not have come up with. Holding complexity is a form of healing and it's also a benchmark of it.

Lines are being drawn in this country, sisters. Neighbor-against-neighbor lines. The issues are significant, many of them serious enough to determine future life on this planet. I want to encourage you to trust yourself, trust yourself like your lives depend on it… trust yourself, do your deepest synapsing, and live your most courageous and authentic lives… and I encourage you to resist black-and-white thinking—to challenge it when and where you experience it. To see it as a danger and assault on your freedom.

You know, Bernice Johnson Reagon, founder of Sweet Honey in the Rock, said, "If you're in a coalition and you're comfortable, you know it's not a broad enough coalition." Sisters, I believe she was talking about this very thing. Being an activist and fighting against that rigid, binary thinking. I believe she was talking about working with people who were on the right side of one issue, but who were ignorant and/or arrogant as hell on other issues. But she did not say, "Dump the coalition." She was telling us that, when we feel that "I don't think I can stand this another minute," to know that

THIS is the real deal. THIS is coalition. THIS is the work. And it will strengthen a movement and it will grow us spiritually and it will strengthen our sense of self.

We are living in extraordinary times, with unprecedented dangers, but also unprecedented opportunities. Sisters, we all need a bigger synaptic boat.

Blessed be.

Sermon on Dying Well

Okay, Sisters, before I tell y'all what I'm talking about today, I want you to remember that time—if this is part of your story—that time when you first started to realize you might be lesbian, and—if this is part of your story—it scared you to pieces. And if this is part of your story and you do remember, I want you to imagine how you would have felt about going to hear someone get up and talk about being a lesbian. I'm guessing most of y'all would have felt like that was the last thing you wanted to do.

But here's the thing, if you had been scared of being lesbian, but somehow you had let yourself go hear that speaker anyway, it is very likely you would have come away feeling less scared, less alone, more confident, more like "maybe this is going to be a huge adventure instead of a nightmare." It might have helped you understand that your fear was the result of believing what the hetero-patriarchy had taught you about women who love women.

So… keep that example in mind—even if that isn't your story. Keep in mind that hearing about subjects that are scary can actually make them less scary.

And why am I telling you this? Because today we are talking about dying. Not death, because I don't know anything about death. You kind of have to have died to talk about death, and I don't know anyone who died and came back to talk about it, except in myths and stuff like that. I know there are some people who were technically dead for a few minutes and then they came back, and they have written about a tunnel and a white light and seeing people they loved who had already died. I know that lots of folks have reported similar experiences… so maybe there is something to that, but it's so close to dying, it doesn't seem like really reporting on being dead.

Anyway… whatever. I am not going to talk about death, but about dying. Because that is something that people *can* know something about, and because it is something that can go on for a long time. I'm not talking about that thing people say about how "we all start dying the moment we are born," because I think that's kind of disrespectful to the folks who are *literally* dying, whose body has begun a process with terminal illness. So when I say "dying," I'm talking about that process, after a diagnosis that is terminal.

So that's a scary subject to most people. We don't want to think of it. You ask people about their idea of a good death, and a lot of them will say it's a death that is sudden, unexpected, and painless. What they are actually saying is that a good death is one that will not entail "dying." Just, boom, before you have time to even *think* it, you're dead.

I want to talk about this because I am sixty-six now and I have begun to experience folks in my age cohort beginning to die on a pretty regular basis. And I understand that this is going to become more frequent as I continue age... unless I happen to outlive everyone I know. But anyway... I am seeing more and more death, and, sisters, most of these folks are not dying well. *Most of them are not dying well.* And these are not just those folks who go along to get along. I'm talking about lesbians and feminists and activists, women who lived and loved passionately and against the grain. I'm talking about women like myself, like you. Sisters, they are not dying well and that worries me. And that's what I want to talk about today. Is anybody dying well, and what does that mean, anyway—"dying well?" Can we learn it? Can we buy it? Can we teach it to each other?

Remember how I started this sermon... talking about avoiding the subject of lesbianism, because it was so scary? Well, the subject of dying is kind of like that. It's scary because of what the mainstream believes about dying. The mainstream culture in the West is actually "death phobic." But what if we challenge that attitude and the assumptions that go with that phobia, like we do with almost everything else? What if we get all radical—down to the roots—about dying?

So today, sisters, I am talking about dying, because I want to see if we can lessen our fears about it, and in lessening our fears, I am hoping that we can get a little better perspective

216

and feel more confident in our ability to make good decisions about dying.

Well, all right. Here we go: What is "dying well?" That's going to be different for everyone. Just like the question, "What is living well?" "Living well" for some people involves raising a family and putting that at the center of their decisions. For other people, "living well" means pursuing an artistic life, making the most of a talent or a vision. For others, it's about a career, or a hobby, or travel, or activism, or community, or a religious or spiritual avocation. There is no set formula for "living well." Everyone needs to determine that for herself.

What we *can* do is look at some of the things that are *not* "living well," or that might get in the way of "living well." One of these is living a life that your parents or other people want you to live. Odds are, that's not going to be your best life. It might be, but probably not. Living to appease your fears is another not-good formula for living well. People who live fear-based lives can end up focused on making money, or trying to move up in terms of class... things like that. Most likely those are not passionate goals, but desperate or unthinking ones. "Living well" pretty much means you have to define what success and security and happiness mean for yourself, and then go after them in your own distinct way.

So, this also applies to dying well. All this dependence on what other people think or believe can really get in the way, making it pretty tough to die well and on your own terms. Well, as much "on your own terms" as the dying will let you... I mean... we're talking about dying here. Maybe a better way to put it would be "finding a way, on our own terms, to accept a whole ton of things about the end of our life that are absolutely *not* going to be on our own terms."

So that's some of what we are going to look at today, and, sisters, I have to say, as lesbians we have a real advantage. We have already made up our minds to live against the grain in a pretty substantial way. We have built some mental muscle in terms of thinking for ourselves and challenging the status quo. If you are reading this Lesbian Tent Revival Sermon, you already know how critical it is to synapse radically and comprehensively. So, we have a little bit of a head start in this "dying well" thing, and we should take advantage of that.

So... all right. First off, I want to say I owe a whole lot of what I'm talking about today to a book called *Die Wise* by Stephen Jenkinson. The subtitle is "*A Manifesto for Sanity and Soul.*" Stephen Jenkinson is a professional grief counselor, and a pretty radical one, from what I read. And he's fairly courageous and articulate in speaking out about what he's seeing. He doesn't romanticize or sentimentalize or sterilize or horrible-ize or Disney-fy or transcend the subject of dying.

So, with a tip of the hat to Mr. Jenkinson, here we go…

First, there are two assumptions about dying that are pretty universal in the medical world. Let's take the first one: "If you can, you should." That means if the technology or the pharmacology for something exists, and if you or your insurance company can pay for it, then you absolutely should do it. The treatment/drug/procedure may be toxic, it may be risky, it may cause complications or trigger a cascade of side effects… but if you can, you should. Period. Because… well, because doing *something* feels like control. It feels like you are doing something. It kind of stokes the engine of hope, which (Jekinson again) can become some kind of "anaesthetic of the spirit" that keeps us from learning to die well until it is too late. And, never let us forget, doing that "something" is going to generate profit for somebody. The medical model for treatment of terminal illness is really set up to do something— actually, a lot of somethings. It assumes that, "If you can, you should" and it will assume that you will also share this assumption. So hold that thought.

The second assumption about dying in the medical world, and even beyond, is this: "More time is always a good thing." And these days almost everybody in palliative care gets "more time." The medical world assumes that is always a good thing, and that everyone will and should want it, and that it is the doctor's job to attempt to provide it. Decisions for treatment are made based on this assumption that the patient will, of course, want more time.

What they don't help patients understand is that "more time" will most likely not be what they think it's going to be. First off, the patient has never lived under the shadow of knowing that they are going to die from what is afflicting them. That's new. The "more time" they will be getting will be time lived with a diagnosis of terminal illness hanging over them. That's different. It's one thing to think, "Yeah, yeah, I know I'm going to die... *sometime*." It's another thing to know, "I have only six months, maybe at best a year to live." So that's a whole different kind of time, living with that understanding. That's living with some inevitable sadness and grief, and some new fears and uncertainties.

The doctors don't really help the patient explore that this "more time" may involve serious dependence on prescription drugs... opioid addiction, for instance. What will that mean to someone whose entire life has been lived in the light of recovery from addiction? What does "more time" mean when it will be lived heading backwards into the attitudes and behaviors of a practicing drug addict? How would that affect a partner in recovery? What does "more time" mean if one is high as a kite, sedated, or numb during all of it?

They also don't help patients consider that "more time" may be time lived chasing after medications and treatments to deal with an ever-increasing array of side effects from ever-proliferating medications and procedures. The medication to treat a side effect may produce its own side effects, and they may require a different medication, which, again, may produce yet another side effect. And so on. This is the reality of a whole lot of this "more time." It's not time spent splurging on some fabulous bucket list of world-class adventures. In the words of Mr. Jenkinson, more time, even in spite of the sedation, can still entail the patient being "vaguely, chronically distraught." *Vaguely, chronically distraught.* There's no pill for that.

Again, in the words of radical grief counselor Stephen Jenkinson, "more time" can mean more time to live dying: more symptoms, more drugs, more weakness, more diminishment, and more dependence. *More dying.*

Sisters, I have seen women I love spending months and even years in this "more time" limbo, and I am pretty sure they had no idea it would look like what it did. And this is one of the reasons why I decided to talk about this.

So… two assumptions about dying that we need to *not* take at face value: "If you can, you should" and "More time is always a good thing."

Now, sisters, I'm not saying that these are always wrong. There are many times "if you can, you should"… especially toward the front end of the diagnosis. And there are many times that "more time" can be a very good thing. Just not always. "More time" can have absolutely no resemblance to what you think it's going to be when you sign on for some plan that's going to give you that. It is *never* going to mean a resumption of the life you have been leading. That ship sailed when you got the terminal diagnosis. So, sisters, we need to be able to think critically about both of these assumptions, because nearly everybody in the medical world will be operating out of them.

It's just like what we said earlier about living well. Sometimes it can be helpful and productive to listen to what other people think we should do. And sometimes it's not.

It's the same with dying well. We have to have worked out our own ideas about what that means… and dying well is a highly individual thing. But we have to have worked out the meaning of our death, before we can really take a real clear-eyed look at "if you can, you should" and "more time is a good thing."

So what is "dying badly?" Again, I am going to look to Mr. Jenkinson, who has seen a huge amount of bad dying. He says it is to "die without dying." Think about that for a minute, sisters. Just wrap your synapses around that. How can you die without dying? What does that even mean? Well, you can be killed. That sudden, unexpected thing, like falling off a cliff. You can die without ever knowing that you are dying. Or you can die hating death and treating it like some kind of enemy to vanquish—an enemy you fight every inch of the way, until you can fight no more and collapse in defeat. You can die refusing to die. As Mr. Jenkinson says, you stop without ever coming to a stop; you end with no ending; you are gone without ever leaving. That's dying badly, sisters.

But the system is set up for these bad deaths: cope, hope, and dope. It never knows when to stop. Or how to help us know when to stop.

And let me say a word here about objectivity, which in the medical world, is called "therapeutic neutrality." Everyone acts like it's a good thing. Therapeutic neutrality is not emotional. It's detached, impersonal, supposedly unprejudiced—which is why we are supposed to trust it. But consider this: What if objectivity is actually a form of prejudice itself? As Jenkinson says, "a view from nowhere." Think about that. A view from nowhere is supposed to be better than the view you see looking out from your own eyes on a world that you spent your life exploring, interpreting and creating, as you look at a death that only you will be dying. The view from nowhere is supposed to carry more weight than the view from all your life experiences and hard-earned lessons!

Jenkinson describes that initial patient consultation, where the bad news is delivered: Three minutes to tell you that you are dying and then forty-two minutes to go over the menu of options for palliative care. Therapeutic neutrality. "If you can, you should." "More time is always a good thing." *As if dying was something that just happens to your body.* I know that sounds crazy, but that's how many folks are approaching it, putting themselves in the hands of our cultural high priests— the medical doctors. Because if all you have is a hammer, everything looks like a nail.

Dying is a profound experience and one that offers unprecedented opportunity. It is a spiritual, psychological, emotional, cultural, and political event. It's *not* just about the body—although, if you follow the Western prescription for dying, it certainly can become that: appointments, treatments, consultations, therapy, prescriptions, schedules. All of that can keep you so busy you can die without dying. Maybe that's the point.

So where does all this death phobia come from? Mr. Jenkinson has traveled all over the world, and he assures us that this terror of dying is far from universal. In fact, he makes a very interesting observation. He notes that it is societies that lack culture who have this phobia around death. Absence of culture: customs, arts, social organizations, histories of achievements. He says that death phobia is an inherited trauma that comes from not knowing how to be at home in the world. It is an inherited trauma from people with no roots in the world, *no sense of indebtedness for what has gone before.*

Sisters, this speaks directly to my lesbian heart.

The mainstream media certainly churns out what appear to be cultural artifacts: films, and video games, and all kinds of music and dance and visual arts. But, as any lesbian feminist can tell you, mainstream media does not represent all of us. It has an agenda that is not necessarily to serve the psycho-spiritual needs of the people, *all* people. It has a bottom line where that agenda should be, and it is a financial one.

That was the magic of the lesbian-feminist movement of the 1960's and 1970's. We realized that we needed a culture that was our own and we invented it. In the words of Monique Wittig, "Failing to remember, invent." We spent out lives inventing and propagating and celebrating a culture that reflected the values we wanted to live by. And, yes, we did worship our ancestors. For many of us, we realized that our tribe was not our families of birth, but the lesbians who came before us. We set about discovering our heritage, reclaiming our forgotten lesbian foremothers, and we did it as if our lives depended on it. Turns out, they did.

Today we can see the legacy that these women left and that we have become a part of, and because of that, we can see the legacy that we are leaving for the lesbians who follow us. We see for ourselves the kind of immortality that we have created for our foremothers in our culture. And, in terms of the body, as we have invented ways to culturally celebrate and commemorate menses and childbirth and menopause, we will celebrate and commemorate our deaths.

We don't need to be dependent on the purveyors of bad dying, because we DO have a culture that is our own. In our days and months and hours of need, let's not throw away this incredible treasure and what it can mean for us as we look for our particular version of "dying well."

One of my most poignant memories of the Michigan Festival was at the Healing Circle on that last day… where women in need of healing lay on the grass with a circle of hundreds of women around them, singing sacred songs. And I remember seeing a woman at the very end of one of these Circles. She was standing up and turning around in very slow circles, her head tilted back to face the sky, with her arms reaching up. She appeared to be in her forties, and she was dying—in the final stages of some terrible wasting disease. Watching her, I wondered if she had helped build the Festival decades earlier. I wondered what her history, her lesbian history, had been. She was saying good-bye, good-bye to something that she treasured, something sacred. Looking at her, I understood that this would be her last year at the Festival. She was not crying. She looked as if her heart was filled—blissful—even as it was breaking. And she was celebrating both.

Sisters, in that moment, this lesbian was dying well. She was dying perfectly. She was in the epicenter of a beloved community and culture, and she was taking it all in, even as she was giving it all up. She was not clinging and clutching to the life she had had before she was dying, holding so tight that it had to be torn out of her fingers bit-by-bit until nothing was left but a meaningless routine of procedures and drugs. She had come to the Festival as a dying woman. And she was living her dying outdoors, among her lesbian sisters. She was living her dying out in the open, in nature, eyes wide open, arms wide open.

In the words of Stephen Jenkinson, she was being "wrecked on schedule." She was not denying and fighting death like an enemy. She was not desperately engaged in pretending to "live a normal life"—that elusive thing that doctors tell you to go home and do. She wasn't waiting to engage with her death until the last experimental drug or heroic procedure had been tried and abandoned, and she was helplessly bedridden, utterly toxic, wasted, sedated and defeated—facing her death as a last resort. She was "wrecked on time," while she was still alive and alert enough to be making and sharing the meaning of her life by participating at the Festival. And look! Here I am writing about her dying and here you are reading about it. I—and this sermon—have become part of her lesbian legacy, part of what her life meant, part of her giving back.

As Jenkinson notes, this "death phobia" of Western culture results in dying that is an "uninformed mania," and endurance test. We lesbians can do so much better than that.

Sisters, of all the radical things in this book *Die Wise*, this is the most radical thing... Listen up:

Suffering... knowing how to suffer, is how you make meaning from what seems random, chaotic, pointless. Wrestling, sisters, *wrestling* is how we do it. Not fighting, like you would with an enemy, an executioner. But wrestling with a worthy opponent, wrestling—like a kind of dancing, with an angel. When you fight something, you make no place for it. You hold it off, you try to exterminate it. When you wrestle, you make a place for it, a proper place. Now, listen to this, sisters, because here it is: *Meaning comes from wrestling*. Consider taking that in... consider easing into a hot tub full of "meaning comes from wrestling." Consider soaking in that until it goes right through your pores. "Meaning comes from wrestling."

Because that's going to be the touchstone of dying well: meaning. What shall your life mean? What shall your dying time be for? GET YOUR DYING TO TELL YOUR LIFE STORY. When your metabolism stops, that should be the least of it.

Because, sisters, if you don't answer those questions, the med-tech world will answer it for you. That med-tech world will tell the story of your dying as a "manageable metabolic event." Thank you, Stephen, for that. It will be a story that is 100% preoccupied with pain and symptom management. It's going to be all about the body, and what's going on with you emotionally and spiritually will be treated, literally, as a side effect. And you can bet that there's going to be a drug for that.

Dying should change everything. In the current model we have for dying, the optimal outcome for treatment is that the patient should be "living a normal life"… in other words, carrying on as if they were not dying. That could be either from denial or acceptance, and Mr. Jenkinson asks us to ask "are those really helpful terms?" If we accept death or deny it, is that going to help us with dying well? Does that terminology just keep us locked into dying as something that happens to us… not something that we can approach as a right, as an obligation, as a political act, as an act of love, as a form of spiritual activism?

Seriously, what does dying ask of us? Surely more than acceptance or denial. Your way of living, and that will include your way of dying, will become part of the meaning of life for others.

Everything else in the plant and animal world leaves behind the elements of their body to enrich the soil, to nurture new life. To be consumed. Except humans. We leave ash or a body so permeated with formaldehyde that, even if our coffins weren't forever sealed impermeably, would poison the ground.

So what can we leave to feed the life that will go on after we are dead?

So let's look at two folks who made a point of leaving a legacy of their dying. One was Greg Allman. He was dying of cirrhosis of the liver, and he made an album called Southern Blood. It's all about dying. He's got "Going, Going, Gone" by Bob Dylan on there, and he's got "I Love the Life I Live" by Willie Nelson. And he's got a song on there that he sings for his brother Dwayne, who died decades earlier, in his early twenties. Greg Allman took his dying and made art out of it, art that was consistent with his living. He sang his dying and left that to the world.

And then there is Oscar Hammerstein who wrote the song lyrics for some of the most beloved musicals of all time: *Oklahoma!*, *Carousel*, *South Pacific*, *The King and I*, and *The Sound of Music*. That last one, *The Sound of Music*, he wrote while he was dying of stomach cancer. He wrote it from his bed. And if you pay attention to the lyrics, they are all about dying... very different from Greg Allman's choices, because they were two different people having two different experiences. Look at the opening of lyric of the title song, "The Sound of Music:"

My day in the hills
Has come to an end, I know
A star has come out
To tell me it's time to go
So I look and I wait and I listen
For the voices that urge me to stay
Yes I look and I wait and I listen
For one more sound
One more thing that the hills might say...

And there is "My Favorite Things," about raindrops on roses and whiskers on kittens—things a dying man in pain chooses to focus his thoughts on. And "Edelweiss"... an even simpler lyric: just one tiny wildflower that "small and white, clean and bright," and that looks happy to the observer. "I Have Confidence" and "Climb Every Mountain"... songs about dying. And the play is about the *Anschluss*, the terrible annexation of Austria by the Nazis... invading and occupying like a cancer—but right in the middle of all this horror and chaos, there is a sanctuary and there is goodness in the human heart, and there is a flight up into those mountains that are so alive with the sound of music. Hammerstein died well, leaving us the legacy of this beautiful musical that is filled with clues about how we can die well also. Deep appreciation for the wonder and beauty of life and songs of courage for the journey. Hammerstein was so clearly wrestling with the angel.

The medical and technical model focuses on what to do about dying. It does not look at what dying asks of us. What and how will our dying feed the life that continues? How can we—and our dying—become part of the meaning of life for others? Jenkinson reminds us that we will not change what our dying means by fighting it like an enemy.

Dying doesn't need to be traumatic. We are living in a time when scenarios of horrific pain are a thing of the past. It is the death-phobic culture that makes dying traumatic. It's the most natural thing in the world. Literally.

And while we are naming the cheats... here's another one: Quality of life as defined by being masterful and competent. As a culture, we are addicted to competence and control. That's why we treat the disabled and the aging the way we do. Consider the price we pay for competence and control addiction... personally and as a planet. And consider, in our dying well, how losing our competence and losing our control could actually be considered a form of deliverance from terrible addictions. Remember, competence is actually the opposite of struggle... and how do we forge meaning? Through struggle. Embrace the incompetence!

How do we suffer well? With collapse and courage. Sisters, it takes guts to stop trying. And it also takes guts to be "wrecked on schedule"—to collapse while there is still time for clear thinking, clear and heartfelt talk. In the words of *Die Wise*: to die "lucidly, deliberately, purposefully, surely and wisely."

Sisters, I don't want to trivialize what it means to lose everything we know, which is what death does. That's huge. And heartbreaking. But let's not decide that the best way to avoid heartbreak is to have less heart. Because that's a very real option, and that's what some of my friends who died badly chose to do. They died on a boatload of sedatives and anti-depressants and experimental drugs. Less heart equals less heartbreak.

No. Let us not compromise our capacity to suffer. That's such an important thing, I'm going to say it again... Let's *not* compromise our capacity to suffer. Remember, that's how we create meaning. And I'm not talking about physical pain here. Nobody is recommending physical agony. I'm talking about the losses, the heartbreak. Sisters, make room for it. Let's learn to grieve. As Jenkinson says, being "heartbroken is not a diagnosis; it's a skill... It's a love affair in reverse."

Just like living a lesbian life, there will be challenges. We will need to take risks. Remember how we had to challenge the social protocols? How we had to talk about our girlfriends and our lesbian culture even when it would make everyone in the room uncomfortable? Remember how we had to risk our friendships to tell folks what was really going on with our lives? Remember how we had to go up against whole institutions... churches, schools, our own government, just to assert our right to our truths? And we also had to risk looking foolish, looking awkward, not getting it right… because we were having to learn a whole new set of values and skills.

Yep. Dying is going to be like that, and it's going to have the same reward: It will be yours. It will be full of meaning. You're going to have to break the deathbed etiquette of just discussing symptoms and medications… or else pretending that you are living the same life you did before you were terminally diagnosed. You're going to have to risk friendships by bringing your whole self, your whole truth to the relationship, and asking them to engage with your dying. You're going to have to lose that deference to the temple of medicine and its high priests. You may have to challenge your religious institution that is holding out those robotic arms to comfort you. And you are going to have to learn to do something you've never done before and that you probably have rarely seen done well.

Jenkinson says that dying wise will entail teaching people how to love someone who is leaving. That's tough. Most of us want to fire people before they quit. And it's also teaching the person who is leaving how to love life… even as she leaves it.

But grief is in the natural order. In the wise words of *Die Wise*, it's not a feeling; it's an understanding. It's being a faithful witness of how it has been with us. Unfortunately, grieving is not inevitable. We need to learn to do it, and we need to teach

each other. "Grief is a way to love what has slipped from view."

It is all about the heartbreak. But listen to Oscar Hammerstein. This is the second half of the lyric to "Sound of Music:"

The hills are alive with the sound of music
With songs they have sung for a thousand years
The hills fill my heart with the sound of music
My heart wants to sing every song it hears
My heart wants to beat like the wings of the birds that
*   rise from the lake to the trees*
My heart wants to sigh like the chime that flies from a
*   church on a breeze*
To laugh like a brook as it trips and falls over stones on
*   its way*
To sing through the night like a lark who is learning to
*   pray*
I go to the hills when my heart is lonely
I know I will hear what I've heard before
My heart will be blessed with the sound of music
And I'll sing once more

Let's choose to really live our dying. Like Oscar Hammerstein, let's cultivate that appreciation for the extraordinary mystery of ordinary things. Let's cultivate wonder. Let's not die confused, devastated and in a state of that "uninformed mania." Let's ask the big questions, the great questions, about life. Finally, "Knowing death well will not inoculate you against mystery, suffering, fear, or resentment. It makes you able."

Blessed be!

www.ingramcontent.com/pod-product-compliance
Lightning Source LLC
Chambersburg PA
CBHW061347280526
45784CB00001B/161